One Lifetime is Not Enough

D1678455

One Lifetime is Not Enough

REX NELSON GREENWALD

One Lifetime Is Not Enough!
Copyright © 2021 by Rex Nelson Greenwald All rights reserved.

No part of this publication may be reproduced, stored in a retrieval system or transmitted in any way by any means, electronic, mechanical, photocopy, recording or otherwise without the prior permission of the author except as provided by USA copyright law.

The opinions expressed by the author are not necessarily those of URLink Print and Media.

1603 Capitol Ave., Suite 310 Cheyenne, Wyoming USA 82001
1-888-980-6523 | admin@urlinkpublishing.com

URLink Print and Media is committed to excellence in the publishing industry.

Book design copyright © 2021 by URLink Print and Media. All rights reserved.

Published in the United States of America

Library of Congress Control Number: 2021912205
ISBN 978-1-64753-842-2 (Paperback)
ISBN 978-1-64753-843-9 (Hardback)
ISBN 978-1-64753-844-6 (Digital)

03.06.21

TABLE OF CONTENTS

Chapter 1:	One Lifetime	7
Chapter 2:	Just in Time, Lives Collide	17
Chapter 3:	A Couple of Weeks later	19
Chapter 4:	A Few Weeks Earlier	24
Chapter 5:	Little Mora	30
Chapter 6:	The Resort	33
Chapter 7:	A Little Grandpa History	40
Chapter 8:	Everything Has a Real Start	44
Chapter 9:	Flashback to Confirmation	57
Chapter 10:	The Fish House	59
Chapter 11:	New Life Style	62
Chapter 12:	Tree Swing	68
Chapter 13:	Hilding	72
Chapter 14:	The Road Less Traveled	75
Chapter 15:	Pojken, He talks!	79
Chapter 16:	The First Play	91
Chapter 17:	The Resort Was Humming	101
Chapter 18:	Then Came Tess	110
Chapter 19:	Back to Little Mora -Those People	117
Chapter 20:	The Invite—People Are People	124
Chapter 21:	Emmanuel	141
Chapter 22:	Coy Becomes a Snoop	143
Chapter 23:	Jordan's Bay Part One: The Entrance to Rebirth	150
Chapter 24:	Part 2 Ten Years Later - The Beginning	163
Chapter 25:	The Moment in Time Was Now	169

Chapter 26:	Don't Count Your Time. Make Your Time Count	175
Chapter 27:	Back to the Dock, 1973	188
Chapter 28:	Over to Cabin 7	196
Chapter 29:	The Walk	201
Chapter 30:	Back to Growler's World	208
Chapter 31:	How to Be Happy	211
Chapter 32:	So, How Many Fish Do You Think Are in the Lake?	213
Chapter 33:	Row, Row, Row Your Boat	225
Chapter 34:	Alone Time	236
Chapter 35:	The All-Americans	238
Chapter 36:	One of the Boys	259
Chapter 37:	Resort Fish Fry and Campfire	264
Chapter 38:	Jordan's Bay Part Three – I Love you like a Tomato	269
Chapter 39:	Saying Goodbye to El	278
Chapter 40:	Saying Goodbye to Tess	280
Chapter 41:	One Final Reading	282
Chapter 42:	Jordan's Bay Part Three - More Than a Murmur	285
Chapter 43:	Ending with Beginning	287
Chapter 44:	Ten Years Later – AMEN!	293

CHAPTER 1

One Lifetime

What happens when an enquiring young person crosses paths with an interesting and worthwhile person? They will pursue, examine, follow, and yearn to find that someone with knowledge. Often, and more importantly, a wise person is uncovered. History is filled with wise, anonymous people and it is with profound delight when that person is dropped into life with presence.

Coy, a vigilant young man, carefully stepped on his tiptoes like numerous times before through the kitchen area of the Little Mora Cabin. He was a prototypical, energetic, bright, twelve-year-old boy with distinguishable self-awareness beyond his time and youthful experience. However, he also lived with the restless and impulsive nature all boys and girls of his age possessed while looking for answers. Answers as profound as how we become good people and how we discover the meaning of life.

Coy lived with purpose and focus, with an overwhelming mission to complete whatever pushed him past his comfort zones. He had discreetly entered the Little Mora Cabin and now stood in silence at the center of the small kitchen area, instinctively knowing from past experience the way to his destination even in the shadow of darkness. However, even with familiarity in hand, he was still filled with consternation and contemplation. His acute self-awareness confirmed he did not have a clue what he was doing or why he was doing it. His inquiring mind and youthful exuberance could not and would not be stopped.

Coy felt irreverent, like one of those altar boys who had just smoked a joint in the john. Nevertheless, he continued moving through the kitchen into the bedroom area, making his way directly to where the old man's memoir book was not-so-carefully hidden. His innate presumption told him it must have been left there and hidden just well enough to be found. He pulled the chain on the lamp and turned on the meager light while reaching down and picking up the book with care, knowing it deserved to be treated like a treasured possession which surely stood the test of time.

Coy carefully unwrapped the tie band from the book, which kept the well-worn pages and loose notes from spilling out, and sat down on the edge of the bed near the nightstand. He opened book and set it down on his lap and decided to let God choose where and what was to be read this day. After a brief moment, he started to peruse briskly through the pages and notes of the treasured mystery book, hunting for clues and perhaps unforeseen pearls. He let his fingers, eyes, and mind go to the pre-ordained pages God wanted him to read. He browsed through familiar first few pages and arrived to about the one-third portion of the book. His leading forefinger stopped, and he paused to whisper a needed prayer. He was feeling a twinge of guilt, as if Jesus had taken a swing at him. The prayer calmed his mind. He continued to reflectively examine the words written by an older man and pondered and passionately desired to know the where, when, and how moments in life when the well-traveled timeless words would have been written.

Coy stopped reading every so often to look up and around while straining to hear something hidden in the silence. He listened carefully and looked around for any noise or anyone or anything, as if someone or something else wanted to be in his space.

"Holy cow!" he whispered loudly, as his reflections exploded with too many thoughts. The words and language recorded in the book were difficult to read, understand, and comprehend, and he struggled mightily. He sat silently in thought, hoping the feeling of vulnerability was external, intentionally hiding his internal deliberations.

The story and mystery became vaster and more confusing each time Coy read from the mystery book. His sympathy grew deeper for this older man each time he read from his book. He was entangled with a devotion bordering on obsession for answers that fueled his unquenched thirst to understand this older gentleman, who was dropped like an A-bomb into his life. His young mind cognitively recognized each glimpse with a desire to quench the thirsting of his heart to learn the truth and purpose.

Coy stopped again and looked around the room. He looked at the nightstand and ironically thought how the book was hidden neatly and in view on the lowest shelf. The bedroom was small, with three twin beds and one window that gave barely enough daylight in the room to let him navigate through the book. There was one small lamp on the lone nightstand. The extra effort it took to read the welcomed expressions in the dim lighting invariably enhanced his concentration to read even more carefully and clearly for answers and meaning.

Coy was always pleased to discover the writing to be remarkably legible, albeit faint, but never dull. The wording was difficult for a twelve-year-old and obviously came from a very intelligent and perhaps educated man. Coy prayed silently again for direction and answers, and God directed him to a heading that grasped ahold of his attention. He began to read out loud quietly. The heading was dated April 12, 1961. He had a sensation of a light being switched on inside his head, like a revelation with a strong feeling and belief that this was the perfect place to read. The date was of his birth and his aspiring ambition was rewarded with enlightenment.

April 12, 1961

The existential threat may be life itself. What can possibly give life meaning? I am hoping my story does not begin at the end. Nonetheless, endings are beginnings we need time to recognize. My experience has told me for young and old folks alike, such as myself, there are moments in time where we realize one lifetime is not enough! The finest way to reward a life is to recognize and enjoy lovely moments. Where do we reach the place where justice is done? Oh, how I pray and hope my moment will be enjoyed and give life meaning.

The heaviest charge against this world does not turn upon the things I have done but on those I have not done. I wait for moments that define life. However, countless years have disappeared from me as if I am being spilled like a lonely drop of water in an ocean. My time is passing away with deadly persistence. This continuous life struggle over the limitations of time has truly become a lifetime affair. I struggle with the thought that if I leave my place in

> line, it will be filled easily by another. It scares me to the deepest hole in my soul, to a point where I do not step out of my lifeline, and I stop living life on and with purpose. I look around and observe, and it seems some accept their blessings learned divinely over time. Nobody is meant to be in this exact spot in line meant for them or me. I still stay in my own line with fear. Take the fear away or keep it. Thy will be done.

Coy paused, looked around, and stilled his mind in the silence. He had no other choice but to continue reading.

> A special meaningful moment may not seem salient when they enter any of our life paths. They may well pass without notice if one is not enlightened enough to pay attention at the time. The underlying struggle excites and depresses me at the same time. I desperately desire to have the ability to open my eyes or have the ability to help others open their eyes to the moments that resonate. My conclusion at this point is, that to some, this dedicated effort will become the life that shapes and carries where they are meant to be. To others, the refusal or inability to recognize the moment will desensitize a heartfelt life, like the refusal to hear something that makes no sound no matter how near or frightening and exhilarating. The entrance of a defining moment so often, if it does not come with a big bang, hardens hearts, creating difficult access. Help me soften and open up my heart to the moment.
>
> Life, to some, becomes a pursuit of living with the hope of a desired moment of freedom. Freedom becomes one of life's greatest lies. It gets muddled with pride, habits, duty, dedication, and the almighty presence of the aging process.

The weight of liberty becomes overbearing and debilitating. The aim becomes wearisome and too overwhelming to overcome alone. As you know, I pray to be alone and with people at the same time.

A devoted few attempt to live divinely hard for the chance of any moment. However, it appears many live stuck in the past or live only for a bright, wonderful future with the realization that even if there is a future it might not be wonderful or bright. Nevertheless, we are only guaranteed the present with a future by faith only You can give. People become blind regarding their memories that get exasperated by blurry and habitual vision. It is so unfortunate most are not chosen to be blessed enough to understand and recognize the moments in life that change courses. We wait for a big event in life, in desperate hope, the moment in time will make the difference. Or, even more harshly, we define many moments to be much bigger or smaller than they really are without careful recognition. Nevertheless, life is made up with little twinkles of special purposes within the precious moments of each day. The moments pass by, often without proper notice or proper remembrance. Help me not to pass by moments. If you have chosen me, let me accept the choice.

The forcefulness of unhappiness creeps into my existence and gives me eyes of wood. Such eyes transform the most resplendent of visions into the dreary, lamentable, and unbearable. Somewhere in my life, I want to be that 'Hi Ho Silver' guy who stamps out evil and has happy endings. My vision has become blinded. Give me vision that sees.

"Enter through the narrow gate. For wide is the gate and broad is the road that leads to destruction, and many enter through it. But small is the gate and narrow the road that leads to life, and only a few find it" (Matthew 7:13-14).

The good book tells us... oh... dear Lord, You move in mysterious ways. Fate appears to run its own race.

The narrow path has ostensibly disguised itself from me as narrow opportunities. No one willingly accepts the statement that most seem to want to not get hit with life too much. We insufferably and latently live to not get hit. However, no one wants to get hit too little with life either. We live with the hope the gateway must be wide, and it cannot to be closed without permitting entrance. Wide just has a better feeling than narrow. Some live with blind providence somewhere deep inside the soul where there is a dormant standing post to prevent us from getting hit too much. Eating, living, surviving, and moving forward become life. We try to grow into the wider gate and do not want to accept a narrow gate because we grow afraid that we won't fit through it. Life wears us down. The gentle nudging of realization tells us it is not the narrow gate that bothers us. The real bother is we might not be able to go through it no matter how hard we try or how much we want it. Help me enter and fit through the gate.

Some live it and realize we are all soldiers this side of heaven, fighting against the world that continually aims to hammer us down to narrow the path of enlightenment. The anxiety is exasperated with the timeless fighting against the aging process, which tells us each day, "I am getting older." We all fight the 'where, when, and how to *live syndrome'. At some point, people realize that seventy, eighty, or even ninety-plus years of existence on earth becomes like a small drop of water in an ocean when compared to all of time. Some invited find and enter the narrow gate. Some give up and tell themselves they just do not have enough time to find it. Some realize it is not a choice, even though the moments are freely given to be accepted and received. Help me accept the entrance.*

Fortunately, there is a something down deep in my soul that tells me what life is supposed to be and tells me what I am doing right now in the present may not be the right path. Or, is it? Thank You for giving me an inner voice and desire to aim to be narrow and live with a will to have Your will. Although I know this to be true, my mental battle is overwhelming.

I have been taught and trained not to imagine being a soldier going into battle with the aim of not getting hit very much. The very suggestion is ridiculous. The aim is to not get hit at all, obviously! Yet, I get hit with life. I let it happen. I live as time passes on and feign to toughen up and keep the remnant of inner knowledge and desire disguised and covered up with pure humanness. Help me focus Your aim for me.

I continue to live each day like a soldier going into battle with the aim of not getting hit very much. I struggle with making the commitment to live each day with the built-in exceptionalism only You can give. I am now beginning to realize my aim; life still hits me. Life hits with bullets and arrows of habits and built-in familial, genealogical, societal, and ingrained natural temptations and desires to fit in and be normal. It has become a slow death process while breathing a life away. You have given us a tough trait to overcome. I somehow know every time I say yes to temptations and habits, it will naturally make it harder to say yes to You the next time, all the while missing desired exceptionalism. Help me be tough Your way.

Really? What is the difference with getting hit with one or a dozen bullets? They all kill. It only takes one! However, if it takes only one to be bad, logic tells me it also takes only one to be good. That is good news. When I kill, I aim to kill. Therefore, the logic You have shared with me tells me when I need to aim to live.

Innocence, naivety, and youth are the strongholds I grasp that speak to me daily. Good as they may be, each is hard and impossible to hold. Help me find a way. The easy path should be to give up my strongholds and let go. I pray to be near one special life You put in my path, and together we enter a path of life to help each other overcome. I just hate to admit it. Apparently, it is never done alone. Therefore, I must admit the gate is narrow and, really and unfortunately, only few enter.

Pulled, pushed, side by side, it does not matter as long as the gate is open. Let me enter, dear Lord. That is how it is with life and death. You spill a drop of water from the cup, and the cup remains full.

I am not afraid of dying. I am afraid of being dead. Show me a glimpse. The revelation of the moment becomes final with the realization that the only way to win the fight to retain victory is an embodiment of the thought where the only way to survive and thrive is that one life is not enough. I pray You will not let death melt my pages away. My burning midnight oil is running low and that is it for now.

Coy felt chockfull and his head would not let him read anymore. His brain was exploding in a fire of thoughts and was completely out of energy. Without knowing how or when it happened, he found himself kneeling next to the bed by the nightstand. He realized the position helped with the minimal light from the lamp. With book in hand, he realized he was in a praying position. He found, as of late, he was praying more and more; when in the past, he only prayed when asked to or at church, and rarely did he pray alone. Coy prayed silently and carefully put the wrap band back on the well-worn book, and he put the treasured book right back as close as possible to its original position on the lowest shelf of the nightstand. He stood up and quietly walked on his tiptoes out of the Little Mora cabin.

This story begins around the year of our Lord AD 1973, in northern Minnesota, United States and winds up with eternity.

CHAPTER 2

Just in Time, Lives Collide

Young men can be put into situations where they can move to the next level of maturity in a very short period of time. Coy, an atypically busy, inquiring young man, had all the qualities to make the next step to young adulthood. A great deal was going on in 1973 in the United States of America and in Coy's life. Coy had loving, wonderful parents and one sister. However, his family was in disarray. His mother's mother just passed away, and his parents decided it may be a nice reprieve for them and Coy if he would spend a few weeks at the Lake Esquagamah resort in Northern Minnesota with his father's father during the summer of 1973. This was where this adventurous summer story commenced. Besides his grandfather, Coy developed many relationships at the resort while he was there. However, he built a lifelong eternal relationship with a man known as Growler. Neither Coy nor Growler had any idea of the impact and eternal implication their unimaginable relationship would have on each other. In no way did they anticipate the lasting impact or ending. The apex of their relationship happened just a couple of weeks after Coy was dropped off at the lake resort. Coy knew some day he would have the courage to write down his experience because, after all, one life is not enough.

CHAPTER 3

A Couple of Weeks later

There was not a murmur or movement within the experienced, seasoned hand holding the .357 magnum revolver with perfect authority. Growler pushed the cylinder open and eerily loaded the gun with one bullet, spun the cylinder and closed it in position expertly with precision, while looking directly at the young man he knew as Coy. He lifted the revolver up and pressed the muzzle end near the forehead of the young man he cared for and loved. His tattered, well-practiced hand did not shake at all as he held the gun within an inch of the young man's forehead. Growler was in such a condition he could no longer be identified with pronouns. He was only an object. His stare could turn the sun ice cold, as if he was a direct descendant of the first murderer, Cain.

Over a lifetime, Growler had learned the only way to get away with death was to continually step within an inch of it. Life was to be taken, not given. The young man, of course, did not have the lifetime of experience that was being shattered this morning and sat there speechless and motionless, but with serenity. He looked directly into the old man's bloodshot, well-traveled, deep, bottomless, mossy eyes. The moment was like a wild dream sequence in which danger was all around, and the hero or the villain was frozen and could not move or even have the ability to move a muscle to retreat from the danger. The motionless, spine-chilling moment froze time.

Growler had faded eyes, eyes the color of swamp spume, mossy eyes nobody else in the entire world would care to look out from. The moment silenced everything around them. Life was so quiet, even a drop of water falling into an ocean of water would have been heard. Coy could feel and hear his fingernails growing. The sudden feel of the cool wind blowing across the lake was all that was needed for the feeling that his teeth were burning. Unrecognizable senses and feelings were surfacing.

If Growler's eyes had the ability to speak, each eye could carry a conversation over an entire sports stadium of rabid fans screaming for no other reason than for desperate hope of attention. The irony of timeless stoicism was deeply embedded within those eyes and, along with the deep sagging circles directly under his eyes, he looked so stricken it was like Jesus had taken a swing at him. The weight of life was upon him, so overwhelming with the realization that his weary struggle of a loyal, stoic life might be at its end and outlived. He had outlived his purpose.

Silence was broken.

"Do you believe? Why? Who are you?"

Growler broke the silence and asked the young man as if interrogating. The timbre of his voice reflection was clear as he spat out seven words with his unusual, well-traveled, practiced, and disturbing sputter. Growler had a way of speaking softly and loudly at the same time.

Coy knew his winsome smile would not shatter the strain of the moment, and he remained dour. There was an eternal lifetime of built-up, covered-up anger that could not and would not be squelched with every intention within Growler. Even though his worn-out face and gestures looked more exhausted than earned from a close proximity, there was effervescent intention. Coy stared right into the man's eyes- eyes with the feel and color that men and women take up the sword to follow, the eyes nobody else sees. Coy remained serene, albeit scared beyond comprehension to the point of losing control of his feelings. Still, Coy perceived a sense of compassion. Buttons, that he did not even know were present within his young heart thought process, were being pushed. Coy had a hot, uneasy, helpless feeling, like being inside the belly of an enormous moth near a hot fire, coming over him. His learning and desire to understand gave him surviving and enlightening thoughts, given from an unknown hollow.

Coy, at this exact moment, had compassion a young man could not obtain until kindness had filled him after an entire life of compassion hunting. He had peace somehow and some way, right at this moment of truth with divine providence. Coy did not have time to think, and if he did, he surely would not be able to identify the depth of the ache happening. It was like he had a blister on his instep and a gnat in his eye at the same time. He was starting to sense his total loss of being able to breathe. This was one of those surreal moments in time; twas like gazing over a majestic mountain view, speechless because of the mere unknowing feeling of not being able to describe the overwhelming flow of sensations and emotions.

Too many thoughts raced through his mind at once, like eating an entire box of chocolates just out of spite without tasting the goodness. He had no time for reasoning and thinking. What would happen would happen as a poor or good habit, depending on the one's point of view. Coy's mouth was so dry even a sponge of vinegar would not satisfy. Whatever he could do or say was from the real purposed person within and, in no way, could have been rehearsed or engineered. The hesitation felt like eternity, yet long enough. He was given the strength to respond. He had one simple and stirring response from a depth so deep it was past the inner workings of his own heart.

Coy began chanting clearly and without stumble, "Jesus loves me! This I know, for the Bible tells me so. Little ones to Him belong; they are weak, but He is strong. Yes, Jesus loves me! Yes, Jesus loves me! Yes, Jesus loves me! The Bible tells me soooo." He sang it out with a youthful tone and with tears of joy and fear, just as it was supposed to be sung.

The moment climaxed like a small pebble landing in the center of a perfectly serene body of water, and the ripples became the only defining purpose. The old man's heart, figuratively and with spirit, left his chest and landed at his feet with a bounce, simultaneously with the loss of purpose. His strong grip on the .357 magnum revolver began to shake; his grip collapsed, and the gun fell to the bottom of the boat. His eyes welled from a dry source of forevermore. A marvel within the miracle of realization was happening between these two souls.

Growler did not cry. He did not even have one bead of sweat. He began to speak with pure and clear diction within a second of the collapse. Life hidden with grief had risen and grabbed hold of his heart. His soul was ambushed with emotions, and his lips began to tremble. He was swept into the current of all the potential loss of time. The devil had been fought, no holds barred, boots a-kicking, and eye-gouging permitted. The old man was duly marked and scarred but survived.

"Jesus loves me, this I know, for the Bible tells me sooo..." the old man began to chant. "The best answer ever given, son. Life is not what just happens!" Growler said clearly as he looked intently into the eyes of the young man, with all intention of reaching the soul. The old man became young as if reborn before Coy's sight. His ears were ringing from the past as he could hear his first drill sergeant enter his soul when they were standing nose-to-nose some forty-plus years earlier. "All men die, few men ever really live. After all, you can't change Jesus, for Christ's sake!" Growler hesitated a moment and then continued, "Young man, Winston Churchill once said the most difficult moments and things in life so often can be described by one word." He paused for reflection and looked across the water, then said, "Jesus."

Growler understood. One life is not enough!

CHAPTER 4

A Few Weeks Earlier

The First Day

The early summer morning air in northern Minnesota was already hot and steamy when Coy's parents dropped him off at the Lake Esquagamah resort. They were under the shade of the distinguishable big oak trees at the entrance. It was the usual setting for a northern Minnesota resort. However, this resort was old and beat up, yet with a wealth of character. The caretaker and host for Martha, the owner of the land and the resort, was Coy's grandfather- his father's father.

Coy knew his grandfather as Grandpa. They all stood beneath the shade of the big oak tree at the resort entrance. Coy's mother and father stayed for a brief conversation of niceties, and shortly thereafter headed back home after a good set of hugs. Of course, when you were young, you nested in your parents' plans, not your own. As his parents jumped back in the car and headed out the entrance, Coy already knew he had possibly been bumped out of the nest.

The early morning light sprinkle of rain was the only reprieve from the sauna of the upcoming summer day. Freshness in the air abounded. The humidity and air temperature might have been downright miserable if a young boy's heart would even have wanted to notice. The resort was filling up with summer travelers and city vacationers, like so many of the resorts surrounding the tens of thousands of lakes in Minnesota. Coy had already assumed that most likely, they would be the same people who were always there. The Lake Esquagamah resort was around 120 miles straight north of Minneapolis and had the unique ability to bring city folk and country folk together from Minnesota, Wisconsin, Illinois, and other surrounding states for the singular purposes of fishing and family time in the Northern Minnesota wilderness.

Coy had been at the resort many times before, mostly on opening fishing weekend with Dad and the guys but also weekends with the family and some week-long stints in the past. However, this would be his first time staying for an extended time and alone without his dad and or mom and older sister. The prospect of a summer's long adventure with Grandpa would have been too exciting to bear, that is, if it weren't for the circumstances causing this trip.

Grandma Elma had just passed away unexpectedly two weeks before. Grandma Elma was his mother's mother. It had been sudden without warning. A heart attack was what everyone kept saying. Coy didn't understand. He kept saying to himself, "How and why would someone attack Grandma's heart? She had a big and good heart."

After the news of Grandma's death spread and the funeral passed, all seemed to be in a state of confusion and chaos. Plans and wills and distant family members overwhelmed the household, and his mother, with his father's blessing, decided and agreed it might be nice for Coy to get away and spend some summer time with Grandpa at the lake. A mother's and father's reprieve, after all, was one away from their kids sometimes. Of course, this was all done in love.

Coy found himself dropped off at this northern Minnesota lake resort overlooking Lake Esquagamah. While they met Grandpa at the resort entrance, his emotions, thoughts, and apprehensions were on high alert. In addition, standing next to Grandpa was another unknown man whom Coy immediately judged to likely be a distant family member. The three of them watched as his parents' vehicle went back up the hill and out of sight.

"Coy," Grandpa said as he grabbed his grandson in a tight hug, tight as could be with only one full arm. "Looking good, Pojken, looking good." Grandpa leaned away and rubbed his right temple with his stump of an arm, which had been cut off at the elbow joint and continued. "Let's get over to Little Mora and get you settled in. Then maybe we'll get out on the lake for some fishing later today. I see you noticed this fellow next to me. We call him Growler, and he is one of us and not a bad card player to boot."

Coy was a natural introvert and a bit shy in new situations. He said, "Ya," in response and simply nodded. The stranger didn't say anything, and his communicating expression was somewhere between a smile and a growl. Coy caught himself staring at the strange man with wonder. Coy could not help but prejudge, and prejudge he did. He remembered Mr. Huberty, his science teacher who was from out east somewhere, telling him sometimes he felt like his life was dropped in a wasteland called Minnesota as penitence or something, and this place seemed to be filled with mush-eating nincompoops who communicated with monosyllabic grunts. He said that to

Coy in disgust after giving him some extra credit work, and all Coy could grunt out was, "Ya." Maybe Growler fit the bill. Coy hated when he judged, especially on outward appearance only.

Little Mora was the nickname for Grandpa's cabin at the resort. It was more than a nickname as it was on a painted wood plank mounted above the entrance door. Grandpa was the keeper of the resort. The man was responsible and kept things in order and ran it for Martha, the owner of the resort. The resort was built on Martha's family land, and she lived in the original farmhouse situated on the west side of the resort behind a small wooded area halfway up the hill.

Coy had the impression of his grandpa being a captain or an engineer of the ship, like Kirk or even Scotty from *Star Trek*. He was the person ensuring the ship maintained its course throughout the occasionally turbulent air of a Minnesota summer. Growler might have been in the Federation but from the other side of the universe or somewhere, very likely a non-human alien, Coy imagined and smiled to himself inside.

The hugs, kisses, and goodbyes were finished. Coy's parents had left to get back home to the big city and to their other responsibilities in life. The trio began to walk the brief trek to the Little Mora Cabin, which was tucked snugly northeast from entrance off the main gravel road between the woods and the lake on the far southeast side of the resort. It was not the choicest spot on the resort, but the spot had a purpose, so when new visitors entered off the gravel road, they instinctively knew they would need to check in there. It gave Grandpa easy access to fishing and hunting while keeping him available to the issues inherent to running and being the gatekeeper of the lake resort. Little Mora was the first cabin built and was the cabin where the workers stayed during construction of the other six cabins sometime after World War II. The resort in general and the cabins were now decrepit and downright beat up. However, the fishing at Lake Esquagamah was heavenly, and that trumped the inconvenience of city folk whining about the conditions. Little Mora might have been the first cabin built, but it sure had character. It had its own personality, with a feeling from the past and nuances, including its familiar odor and ambiance.

Coy walked behind the two men. He was now formally introduced to the other man with a handshake while they walked together. As they got close to Little Mora, Grandpa's dog Pretzel came running at Coy and jumped up and licked him in the face. Coy love dogs, and dogs love Coy. Even with that distraction, he could not keep his eyes off Growler as he tried to keep in step with Grandpa. However, carrying his duffel bag, backpack, and his fishing pole made it hard to keep pace, especially when he wasn't watching where he was going. Coy tripped a couple of times over exposed roots and the boggy subsurface, which was a signature of the resort along with a small three-foot wide creek called Chelsea Brook. The creek meandered between the Little Mora Cabin and the rest of the cabins and crossed through in a culvert under the entrance road and around in front of the fish house and off into the woods on the west side of the resort near the shoreline. Coy was too occupied with fascination at the presence of this Growler to pay attention to the simple task of walking.

Coy knew there was something different about Growler, provoking his enquiring mind to action. The stranger instantly captivated Coy and filled him with curiosity. It wasn't his clothing. He wore the same fifties garb as Grandpa. It wasn't his speech. He hadn't said a word. No, it was something else, something deeper, which put Coy's attention on high alert.

They reached Little Mora. Coy vowed to himself he would spend time finding out what it was about this man Growler. Coy felt interested with vexing thoughts.

Grandpa said as they reached Little Mora, "Now go on inside and set yourself up in the bedroom at the bed nearest the door. Then come on out here, and we'll take a walk around the entire resort. We will show you off and around and discuss what you'll be helping with this summer."

Coy replied dutifully with a simple, "Yes, sir."

Coy opened the screen door and stepped through the door into the cabin. Coy looked back to see Growler give a grunt, which judging by what happened next, Coy assumed stood for: "I'll be seeing you later." Growler walked past Grandpa to the north side of the cabin and in the direction of the woods outlining the east side of the resort. The mystery of Growler was gone for now.

CHAPTER 5

Little Mora

Coy's inquisitive mind took over as he entered the dimness inside the Little Mora Cabin. He thought it was like looking at the sun when it dumped itself into the horizon and the rest of the world went blank. He entered Little Mora with familiarity and did a once-over glimpse around the small cabin. In the past, Coy's family would either sleep in a tent or if a cabin was available, stay in one of the other cabins. He never actually stayed or slept in the Little Mora Cabin. Albeit all family activity revolved around this cabin, the cooking was done on the stove inside or the grill by the fire pit, and meals were served out on the small wooden picnic table near the fire pit fifteen feet outside the door. Card and board games were played in the cabin or at the picnic table regularly. Grandpa's 1969 El Camino with a camper topper was parked neatly on the south side of the cabin. Coy had slept in the camper a few times in the past when available cabins with beds and tents were full of family members and other guests. Coy preferred and enjoyed the alone-time sleeping arrangement of the camper, but it was not as much fun when he shared the camper with a cousin or his sister.

Cut-off tree stumps and old lawn chairs surrounded the fire pit in front and on the west side of Little Mora. Little Mora was a small rectangle building of maybe twelve by twenty feet, arranged into two square rooms with a half wall, whose main purpose was to separate the kitchen area from the one bedroom. The kitchen living area had a wooden bench built in and up against the door wall with a table and three chairs on the opposite side where all the eating and socializing, like playing cards, took place. On the one and a half wall separating the main area was a sink, stove, small refrigerator, and cupboards. The cabin did not have running water. It did have electricity. There were two small windows on the south wall. A two-foot by one-foot Franklin stove was positioned near the north wall between the table and the small, more modern cooking stove. The wood-burning Franklin stove was the heater for the cabin. All the cabins had this amenity. There was no indoor bathroom because there was no running water in Little Mora. The two-holer was to the east of the cabin on the edge of the woods.

There were three beds in the bedroom- two side-by-side twin-sized beds, and one small bed at the entrance- with one small nightstand and one small lamp. The responsibility of the person sleeping on the smaller bed was to pull the modified bed sheet across the opening of the doorway to get some privacy from the main room. Coy took the smaller bed at the bedroom entrance as instructed. He only had time for a once-over look; the pictures on the walls and other amenities that needed a closer look would have to wait. He set his bags on the bed as quickly as he could. There was no time to settle in and no need to set out his things now.

CHAPTER 6

The Resort

Coy barely made a pit stop in the cabin. Within just a few minutes of arriving and entering Little Mora world, he was walking with Grandpa around the resort along with the dogs. Pretzel was Grandpa's dog, and Brownie was Martha's dog, but they really were the resort's dogs. Pretzel was a short-haired mutt of some kind with a mix of Basset hound and wiener dog, who had an awesome fun excitable personality. Pretzel had become quite an asset, as he would chase the little varmints out from under the cabins with a distinguishable yelping bark, sounding like a laugh and a growl at the same time. Brownie was a big brown dog that, from a distance, could be mistaken as a small brown bear. Brownie was gentle and liked to sit around with the people and observe the fire at night, as if listening in. Coy would often look at Brownie to see if he was listening and wondered if he heard, felt, or understood the meaning of it all like humans.

Grandpa walked at a slower and easier pace and Coy could keep up by his side without much effort.

Grandpa showed Coy the resort while explaining responsibilities, chores, and introducing his grandson to the community of vacationers who were not fishing or in their cabins. He gave him a rundown of the new folks coming in and who was leaving and bits of history about them all. Albeit, the conversation was mostly one way. Coy was mesmerized and thoroughly enjoyed being with his grandpa. Coy had a built-in respect for Grandpa and always looked up to him as a person. Grandpa shared what he knew and explained the history of the folks while explaining directions and chores. The conversation was becoming more muddled to Coy by the minute, and all he was hearing was, "They're from Minneapolis somewhere," "They're from somewhere near Chicago," or "I am not sure where they are from..." It was like listening to a slow love song on one of those radio stations Coy did not listen to. However, he always tried to listen intently knowing anything Grandpa had to say was worth a listen.

While Grandpa was leading and explaining, Coy recalled that the resort stretched out around a quarter mile, like a giant beach around the southeastern shoreline of Lake Esquagamah. Later, Coy would deduce the resort was positioned like a starting line and looked like an entrance or gateway to the lake. It really had a very welcoming look. On the east end of the beach was Cabin 1, with Little Mora directly south between Cabin 1 and Cabin 2 and on the south side of Chelsea Brook and within eyeshot of the road. On the west end was Cabin 7. There were campsite spaces west of Cabin 7, where campers and tents were situated on the mowed and cleared out area all the way to the far west tree line. Martha's house was not in clear view from the cabins and was not built close enough to the shoreline to have a view. Looking out across the lake were the surrounding woods that hugged the resort like a wooded blanket, concealing the resort from the real world. There was a radio tower with a blinking red light on top of the high embankment on the northeast shoreline of the lake; it was mesmerizing to look at from the fire at night.

Grandpa told Coy the resort was on about ten acres. The actual clearing from the surrounding forest and the road for the cabins and camping was around three acres. It did not really take that long to walk the entirety. One south side of the resort and on the other side of the woods from the resort was the road, and there was what appeared to be a little white building straight west and up the gravel road on top of the big hill. Coy couldn't quite make out the white building's vague location as his grandpa led him around the resort. Coy would learn the best view of the white building on the top of the hill was from the lake around the corner through the narrow passageway into the bay called Jordan's Bay. When they reached the first of the seven cabins, Coy thought he needed to explore the western woods when he could break away from Grandpa and all these new duties and responsibilities.

The cabins were arranged and numbered 1 through 7, with Cabin 1 on the far east and Cabin 7 on the west side of the resort along the lake shoreline. The cabins were not in a straight line, as some were facing the lake directly, while others at different angles. None of the cabins were identical in structure, as if they were just built with no plans but only for convenience of location and with whatever materials available. However, each cabin had all the basic amenities. The cabin numbers were on the top corner below the fascia line of the sloped roofs, hidden discreetly near the entrance doors. Coy and Grandpa reached the west side of the resort. The first cabin they came upon was Cabin 7. Grandpa continued with instructions. Coy looked to the west and counted three push-up tent trailers, five tents, and two large Winnebago-type campers.

He turned around and watched Grandpa examine the cabin and the surrounding landscape in his normal discerning and thoughtful way.

"Okay, let's figure this out, Pojken," Grandpa said in a strong voice bordering on dictatorial. "At the cabins, we have jobs to complete daily and weekly. You will lend a helping hand and have some responsibilities, such as getting and splitting firewood for the fire pits and the wood stoves, making sure the grass is trimmed from the cabin to the cabin's dock, and cleaning the windows once a week or so and, of course, delivering the laundered bed linens when needed." He stopped and rubbed his right temple with his stump of an arm and continued, "and also a big responsibility is to be a good steward, throwing in some social direction. On the other hand..." he slowed for a moment, then continued, "Martha does a pretty good job with that."

Coy's mind was racing and thinking, but he was a little confused why Grandpa called him Pojken again, as he really did not know what a Pojken even meant.

Grandpa pointed with his stub of an arm as he spoke, while motioning in the direction of each of the prospective tasks. Coy literally sensed the whole arm present as he pointed. Years ago, when Coy was younger, seeing his grandpa work with one arm was scary. After all, the sight of a real one-armed man was straight from one of those horror films his mother would never let him see, as she did not want her young son to have nightmares. Nevertheless, one of a mother's main jobs was to help her offspring be in the presence of good and non-scary situations.

One Lifetime Is Not Enough!

Coy in time had come to see his grandpa as a strong and kind man, and by no means an invalid or scary. Grandpa could do nearly anything, usually better, a two-armed man could do. It was as if having one less arm made him stronger or at least more determined to be able-bodied than any able-bodied man. Coy would have loved to have known his grandpa when he was in his prime of life. He knew even if he had not been related to him, he would have wanted to be his friend.

Coy wasn't really paying attention while they meandered over to Cabin 6. He was too busy wondering and trying to remember the story of how Grandpa had lost his arm to be paying attention. But it did make him think about being born with only one arm. He remembered a mention of a farm accident way back, and he wondered how that all happened. Grandpa could see the daydreams and wonderings forming behind the golden-brown eyes of his twelve-year-old grandson so he called out, "So, you are the dreamer and thinker I remember. Come on, daydreamer, there's still work to do." Grandpa spoke as he looked at Coy. Coy was beginning to realize most of Grandpa's communication was by voice and facial inflections, along with pointing and directing. Coy acquiesced and accepted the communication from Grandpa and thought how that missing arm was just another mystery to solve.

Even though Cabins 6 and 7 were the last cabins built, they had the same weathered and worn-down condition as the other cabins. Each cabin had the same things to be done for them as Cabin 7, but they also had specific upkeep tasks that Coy and Grandpa would tackle throughout the summer. Cabin 5 had a leaking roof, and they would need to work on the floor in Cabin 2 as well as other things. As they reached the resort road, it was beginning to look like Coy would have a busier summer than he had hoped., It went from the resort entrance off the gravel road entrance to the lake and turned down the slight slope and went directly into the lake which was the boat landing. The road and boat landing separated Cabins 1, 2, and 3 from Cabins 4, 5, 6, and 7.

They were now standing near the boat landing. Coy took a prolonged, expansive look out at Lake Esquagamah. He was trying to get a panoramic glimpse into what made this lake, this one of ten thousand of lakes in Minnesota, so special to the vacationers and so important to Grandpa.

Coy thought Lake Esquagamah was a relatively average and ordinary looking northern Minnesota lake, but it was *their* lake. The water was not clear and had a green tint. It looked exactly as one would think any lake full of water and surrounded by trees would look. Coy knew while the water was not clean and clear as expected, the fishing was extraordinary. The lake was river-fed off the Mississippi river waters, which helped bring a brimming list and whole host of bait-biting fish and made the mucky water nothing more than a nuance. There were crappies, walleyes, and northern pike. But more than anything, Lake Esquagamah was full of good-sized yellow bellies and bluegill sunfish. Coy's mouth began to drool as he thought about the edible delight of pan-fried sunfish.

"We have a few jobs down here near the water. We help with boat landings, making sure guests get their boats in safely when we're available. You'll also help with securing the resort boats at their respective docks and every night, one of us will go to every dock and check if the boats are tied up to the docks." Grandpa spoke and pointed to the docks with his handless arm. "Also, when the guests come in from a day of fishing, we stay available and help take in their catch if they desire the help. Then, we may clean or at least help them clean their fish. At least, we point them to the fish house."

Coy didn't think any of jobs seemed too challenging. But that last job, cleaning the fish, concerned him. He had never really cleaned fish alone. He had watched Grandpa clean fish a handful of times with Dad and Uncle Hilb. However, he had never held a knife to a flopping fish all by himself without guidance.

Grandpa sensed Coy's reticence and said, "Don't worry, Pojken. Later, after we go out for a few, I'll show you how to do it right. You have nothing to worry about. For now, though, just make a note of these potential duties, okay?"

"Yes, sir," Coy dutifully responded. He was beginning to feel a bit burdened despite Grandpa's attempt at encouragement.

When his parents had dropped him off no more than an hour before, Coy was just excited to be out of the car. He hadn't thought too much about what he would be doing. But now, after hearing Grandpa list of chores, he began to worry. Coy was starting to wonder if he would ever have time to himself this summer. It was, after all, of vital importance he had time to wonder, wander, learn, and explore.

The pair continued to walk along the lake shoreline as Grandpa pointed at the docks and laid out chores. They reached the far end of the resort's lakefront. Grandpa stopped suddenly, as if he had remembered something. He turned to Coy. "You know, we should go talk to Martha. She's going to want to meet the Pojken who will be helping take care of the resort." Grandpa then walked away from the lake toward the other side of the resort, saying, "This is the way."

CHAPTER 7
A Little Grandpa History

Coy saw Grandpa as an extraordinarily self-sufficient man with history.

Grandpa did not need assistance with life duties, as far as Coy could grasp. Coy's grandmother had gone to be with the Lord a few years back after enduring diabetes and other ailments, and Grandpa's choice of self-sufficiency was thrust upon him. So much of life was not a choice, like living as a one-armed bandit and not being an outlaw.

Grandpa and Grandma were parents of three boys and three girls, all within a fifteen-year span, which must have taken its toll, but it really must have worn on Grandma. The pinnacle of perseverance came in the fall of '52, when Grandpa lost his right arm in a thresher machine accident at their small family farm. Grandpa was the thresher machine man in the small middle of Minnesota farm community. He would work it not only for his field, but for all the nearby neighbors. Thresher machines of the late '40s and early '50s had many moving parts with obvious mechanical issues, and it was not unusual for breakdowns and jams to occur. Grandpa, being a natural-born mechanic and engineer not unlike so many farmers of the day, could get anything to run or work, even with shoestrings. He could fix just about any problem with what was at hand. One late afternoon in the fall of '52, going on early evening after twelve-plus hours of threshing, the machine jammed as it had most likely many times on that day. Grandpa, perhaps in a hurry to finish and probably tired and without even thinking, reached into the belt area. Unfortunately, his shirt sleeve caught and his right arm was pulled in and threshed to the elbow. Ouch!

They had little insurance and not a great deal of public help. Losing the farm was inevitable. The accident and the subsequent decisions had to be made assisted in losing the low- income, low-outcome, eighty-acre strip of God's land the family called home. The result, along with the hurt and loss, was to just become another townsfolk family. This new distinction took a toll on the family mojo, especially the children still at home, including Coy's father. The family moved into the town of Mora, Minnesota, and began the existence of just getting by. Coy's father was the youngest and was twelve years old when the farm accident happened. The family did not really talk about it much. Coy suspected it was probably the ugly memories and the hurt of it all that suppressed the history and story.

Shortly thereafter and for several years later, the family had gotten their feet under them; Grandpa and Grandma and all their children survived by working different jobs, hunting for food, and making enough money to make it through with as much perseverance and prayer as possible. Prior to being taken home to be with the Lord, Grandma worked with Grandpa together at the Lake Esquagamah resort and helped take care of the property for a few years. With their kids long gone and with families of their own, working the resort was a good way for Grandpa and Grandma to remain social and feel needed, if only by the complaining city vacationers who needed their fish cleaned or cabins repaired or outboard motors looked at and fixed up.

It was always welcome when family members visited and stayed up at the lake with Grandpa, especially now that his wife and spiritual leader of the whole family passed. Grandpa was an introvert but down deep, he was a people person. He sure enjoyed the company when family and friends showed up. In addition, he had developed strong and deep relationships with patrons of the resort over the years. The resort was not one of the top first-class destinations in northern Minnesota, like the resorts over in the Brainerd area or one of those fancy destinations in the chain of lake resorts of Cross Lake. The Lake Esquagamah resort, a resort with character and history, had a lake that produced all types of fish but most importantly, a plethora of beautifully sized, edible sunfish.

Although there were six other male grandchildren in Grandpa's world, Coy's family liked to fish and visited Grandpa and Grandma at the lake several times a year, but now it was just Grandpa they visited. Coy knew the resort but really did not know the workings. Moreover, Coy was just coming to the age of understanding. There was no doubt Grandpa and Coy had a unique bond and connection, and Growler put a little spark and spunk in the mix.

Coy had some of Grandpa's personality. They both loved dogs. In fact, Coy was named after one of Grandpa's best and favorite hunting dog when his father was about 12 years old. They enjoyed and knew playing solitaire was pretty fun but competing in a good game of Kings-in-the-Corner or cribbage together helped the days pass when there was friendly battering of competition. Grandpa had history, perseverance, and a story; he made life an experience. Since Grandma, his life partner had passed, he had become a very self-sufficient, one-armed man. It was fun for Coy to watch his Grandpa work the cards with his one hand and not miss a beat or a play. This all appeared to be terrific breeding ground for a young boy to learn about life, or at least that was one of the reasons his mother gave for dropping him off for the summer.

CHAPTER 8
Everything Has a Real Start

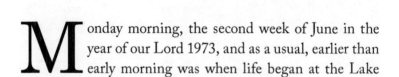

Monday morning, the second week of June in the year of our Lord 1973, and as a usual, earlier than early morning was when life began at the Lake Esquagamah resort.

The Little Mora Cabin light was almost always the first light flicker of life from the darkness each morning. Grandpa, being a little older and worn a bit more, would hug the pillow until 5:00 a.m. or maybe 5:30 a.m. Coy, being a city kid, was not quite used to living the farmer time of Grandpa and Growler. However, after a few days with these two fellows, Coy realized, lickety-split and almost like warp speed, it was time to get up and go when the first glimpse of light entered the dark world of night. Coy, for one, wanted to be one of the boys. Most importantly, Coy did not want to miss out on anything.

Even though Coy fought the early morning routine for a few days or maybe even a week, he adjusted. Coy quickly recognized how nice the early morning really could be with the dew on the ground, the fresh air, and the cool fresh breeze. With the newness-of-life feeling, it was like the whole world was refreshed daily. The worldly, youthful anticipation of the unknown day, the excitement, the learning, the exploring, the growing, the helping, and the forging ahead step-by-step were most exciting at the starting line. Coy learned to appreciate this quality, as he was forced to acquire it or be another forgotten soul. Nevertheless, he really treasured the thought that even the older guys he was bunking up with might still have that same exuberance for life. With the freshness and purity in the air, morning became Coy's favorite time. With certainty, jumping out of bed for it became one of his newly found good memories.

Growler often would wander off and disappear for a while in the mornings, and even Grandpa did not know where he disappeared. Grandpa once told Coy he went into the woods and growled at the world for what it did to him and his life. Coy did not understand Grandpa most of the time, but this explanation was adequate, and he somewhat understood and accepted it. However, full acceptance would require more time and many questions to be answered. When Coy asked Grandpa about where Growler would go in the morning, Grandpa, of course, gave the obvious answer: the two-holer. Coy did not respond but knew there was more.

Grandpa would mumble to Coy a few instructions of what was needed to be done first thing most mornings. Even though Coy knew there was so much area to fill within the Growler mystery, chores had to be done. Coy went about doing his laid-out chores this particular morning, like cleaning and neatening up the fire pit area, checking the fish house, and making a quick check around the resort to, at least, make sure the cabins were there and had not burned down or sunk into the bog of life or something. Coy really did not know what he would have done if there would have been any trouble or issues with the cabins. He did know if there was any trouble, it would most likely be people-related.

Coy got up right with Growler this morning. They, along with Pretzel, stepped out of the two room, no water, no bathroom, bed side-by-side cabin with the usual nuance smell. They made eye contact and gave each other a little pleasant gesture that simply implied, "See you in a bit after we live and do our own things." Coy would always take a quick glance at the mounted walleye above the door on the way out of the cabin, and the caption read, "If I would have kept my mouth shut, I would not be hanging on this wall." Coy went his way, but with one eye looking toward Growler.

Growler had a small carrying bag hanging over his shoulder. He zigzagged across the path, which Coy immediately thought was a technique to keep a foe off his scent or direction. Coy saw him head to the gravel road and start walking westward up the fairly steep hill- the other direction from Martha's house. Coy noticed Growler's walk this morning. He seemed to always walk with purpose. He pushed off his toes like a natural leader by looks and physical actions. Coy had the same walk.

Kids at school would tease Coy and call him tippy toes. Thoughts came to him about what happened this past spring at school. One of the school bullies had approached Coy after physical education class, right after Coy had helped their team win the floor hockey game against the bullies' team in the gym.

"Hey kid, nice goal, but you know what—I really hate you," the bully said to Coy.

"I am sorry, John, but why do you hate me?" Coy responded.

"Because you always walk as if you have purpose, and that bugs the hell out of me," John had said, face-to-face with Coy. John was three or four inches taller than Coy and obviously intimidating. Besides, John had a reputation of being not only a fighter but a winning fighter.

Coy was scared as they both tried to stare each other down. Then Coy broke. "You know what, John? If I can scare the hell out of you, that is okay with me. Maybe a little heaven in there would be nice," Coy said, as he pointed at John's chest.

John hesitated, then said, "Not bad, kid. I think maybe we can be friends after all."

"That would be cool," Coy had responded.

While Coy was daydreaming, Growler disappeared from view. Coy hurried through some of his simple chores. The cabin checking routine would have to wait this morning. He slyly (but not really slyly because he almost had to jog just to walk with Growler normally) had to run purposefully to try to catch up and follow Growler.

Coy's enthusiasm for the unknown and anticipation was peaking. He did not just want, he *needed* to know about this man and what he was up to. The mystery of this man was igniting an excitement he had never experienced. Everyone else in his life was pigeonholed with a description that seemed less like a will of effort but just an accepted way.

Coy did not want to just accept, he wanted to be an exception. Growler sparked his enthusiasm. To Coy, Growler seemed to have depth with exception. From outward appearances and everyone else's opinion, there was just an assumption Growler was a simpleton. Coy thought people wanted to accept Growler for his outward appearance. Coy knew something inside Growler was beyond interesting, intriguing, and possibly really special.

The greatest enemy of love and achievement is the pride in a vibrant young man that tells him nothing is difficult, and he can do anything. Coy walked and talked with confidence, which was one of his strengths yet an annoyance to others in his life. From his first meeting with Growler, he could feel a symbiotic presence. Coy walked and then ran up that gravel road hill with no pride this morning, just curiosity and anticipation.

Why was there always a hill to climb? Always a hill. Coy thought it seemed the important things in life were always strengthened with a hill or a struggle. This hill was placed at just the right place to humble even an energetic young man. Coy reached the top of the hill, with a flat plateau area of about an acre, where a building was meant to stand. There was a neatly constructed white building, which Coy briefly remembered seeing as they drove by it the first day he was at the resort. The elevation rose over the lake and from the plateau, there was a great overview of Lake Esquagamah. It was as if this piece of land, building, and whoever the occupants and patrons of this place would be were all meant to be overseers. There was no shoreline, just a steep sloped decline to the water's edge.

Coy, in a brief respite from the moment, remembered looking up at this area of shoreline from Jordan's Bay when he was out in the boat with Grandpa. He had asked Grandpa at the fire the night before what the white building was for and remembered a murmur from Growler in response before Grandpa said it was just a pretty nice white structure up there on a nice piece of earth. He also said it was like it had fallen right from heaven at just the right place and at just the right time.

Coy had learned his reconnoitering skills from what he had seen on TV. He knew he had to stay back a distance, a technique he learned from watching *Get Smart*. Even though Don Adams played a fool, he always seemed to get the bad guys, and the girl. Even a fool knew when to try to not be noticed. Coy had no gadgets or fun things like a shoe phone, but he did understand he should stay back and hidden, yet close enough to observe. He naturally ended up in a ditch area right at the outskirts of the driveway area, not in the weeds but on the edge of the driveway. He lay down in the grass, which was moist with dew. Coy had a perfect view of the front of the white building. Coy could not help but think the building looked serene and purposeful.

It was around 5:30 a.m., and the beautiful and cloudless sunrise was peeking out at the upper edges of the eastern tree line. Morning dew shone off the surface of the sloped roof of the structure as if heaven itself wanted to make sure there was a reflection. The building had colored windows in some locations and clear panes in others, white siding, and black shutters.

One of the most intriguing features of the building was its entrance structure. There was an overhang where cars could be driven to the front door under the gabled area as steep as a mountainside, which made it look like the building's tail. For Coy, it was like seeing a picture on a wall that would keep him awake with curiosity because he longed to understand what was behind the picture. Coy, as time passed, would have an awakening, like a revelation, to something that unfolded in the story he had not recognized in the picture.

Coy did a double take. He looked at the building again and then again. A light bulb went off in his head. At the building entrance, the overhang structure was held up by a straight support beam perpendicular to the earth and supported with a large post. About three-fourths of the way up from the ground, there was another post or beam structure about the same length, size, and girth that was parallel with the ground. He realized it looked just like a cross, and it was stained a beautiful dark color, which made it stick right out. It shined and glimmered in the morning brightness. Coy realized something without being told or instructed this fine early morning. This was a church. From the road, the facade of the building was inviting, as if the entrance to the building was behind the cross; twas as if the cross was the foundation that held up the entire structure.

Coy was contemplative to say the least this morning. He wanted to be right there in the mix but for now, he knew he was not an invited guest. Coy had a clear view of Growler. Growler stopped near the front door under the structure being held up by the cross, bowed for a transient moment, then did a cursory look around. Coy hunkered down and hid, just in case Growler looked toward the road. The door opened, which surprised Coy as it was very early in the morning. The funny thing was, Growler had not even knocked or made any gesture. A gentleman of around thirty years of age stepped out to greet him. Coy was sweating with anticipation as he struggled to stay hidden and look on. He looked on intently, trying to hear and observe. The thought, "What in the world is going on?" kept pummeling into his temples. His right temple felt like it was going to explode.

The younger, neatly dressed man seemed to have some authority. It looked from Coy's vantage point that Growler showed respect. They seemed to communicate somehow for a moment, then they hugged (a man's type of hug), stopped, and both looked around. Coy ducked down in the ditch. He couldn't hear or comprehend their exchange, but it all seemed odd to him. Growler handed the younger man something, and the younger man appeared to shake his hand, or hand something to Growler. Coy could not see what it might have been, if anything.

They exchanged another communication of some sort. From Coy's vantage point, it did not appear any words were spoken. After just a minute or so, they bowed and lowered their heads together and from a distance, they almost appeared as a silhouette of oneness. Time seemed slow as if it had stopped, yet the moment was very brief. The younger man turned to step back in the building, looked as if he invited Growler in, but Growler's hands gestured a "no" sign. They seemed to understand with communicated silence.

Growler turned and looked around. Coy realized Growler was getting ready to head back to the resort and back to breakfast down the hill. Coy slithered back slowly, as if he was a snake in the grass moving backward. He suddenly had an innate realization this had become a race. Coy finished slithering as far as he could go, then straighten up to his knees and when he was out of sight jumped to his feet in a hunching position and started walking towards the woods. He picked up his pace as he approached the woods knowing that a race was on. He was being careful to not be seen. Growler was no longer within eyeshot and hustled to the woods. Without any forethought, Coy felt he could find his way back down the hill somehow to the resort in the woods and not the road. He knew the road was not an option, so the road less traveled this morning was through the dark woods, down a big scary hill back to home base. He could not understand why, but he was running scared for some reason.

Coy didn't understand why all things had to be a race with him. He felt like a rat in a rat race. Then it dawned on him: something had happened a month earlier. He was with Grandma for the last time. They sat together, just the two of them at the kitchen table, eating some afternoon sandwiches. She spoke about many things Coy would carry with him for the rest of his life. Later, Coy learned at the funeral that Grandma was diabetic, but he hadn't known it at the time they talked. She was told earlier in the year her time was short, and Coy was grateful they he had time together before she died to just talk.

Coy was wet all over from head to toe from crawling and slithering in the wet grass. He now entered the woods with a noticeable panicked pace. The tree branches and undergrowth were all wet, and now he was soaked all the way through to his waist, yet his mind was wandering as fast as his pace.

He was remembering how Grandma would bow her head in prayer before every activity with purpose and good habit. Coy was beginning to realize how that told a great deal about her character. The last conversation Coy and Grandma had was stuck in the mind of an impressionable young man and what she had told him on the last day he saw her alive.

"Coy, the problem with being in a rat race is that even if you win, you are still a rat." He could hear his dear grandma instruct him. Grandma knew her rats, living on a farm her whole life and chasing them in the barn or the chicken coop. Coy felt the race within. However, he realized he was the only rat in the race this morning. Growler was just living. It was not much of a race if the race was all alone.

Coy entered the cover of the woods and started his way down the hill and through the thick foliage. He then remembered what Grandma said when Coy's family departed, giving one last piece of advice. "Dear family, be kind. Remember, everyone you meet is fighting a hard battle." Coy was starting to get it, piece by piece.

He was paying no attention to the task at hand and since the hill was steeper in the woods then the road and the terrain was treacherous, Coy fell three times over rocks, fallen trees, stumps, and a slippery slope of moss- covered boulders as he was fighting his way back to the resort. He found the beaten deer path at the midpoint to the camp, and he knew he was on course. Yet, it was dark in the woods, and it was hard to find his way.

The day felt old already to Coy, even though it was maybe 6:00 or so in the morning. He could feel the heat of the morning sun sprinkle through the tree cover. Even more importantly, the mosquitos, dragonflies, the deer flies with their buzzing, were awake and becoming his sole focus. They popped into the world out of nowhere about the same time each day. Birds were singing, the mourning doves were singing out their familiar mournful, eerie sound of cheer. Squirrels and all the living creatures were squealing and communicating. Coy thought every creature within earshot wanted to be part of the tumultuous yet beautiful morning sound.

It seemed all places and situations had a sound, smell, or feel, and even a blind person would be able to identify where they happened to be at any moment. Early day and early evening, the overwhelming sound was mosquito buzzes, or buzzing flies, and the familiar sound of a wing-flapping dragonfly. Coy learned that dragonflies ate mosquitoes, and even though they seemed a little wicked, he definitely did not want to kill any of them. The small, winding, deer-type path through the thick woods ended at the resort about twenty-five feet behind the fish house. He knew the path, as they buried fish guts back there sometimes and dug up worms and nightcrawlers for bait. Of course, the bears and other scary animals must have known the path also, so even a brave young man was aware of the dangers.

Coy stepped out of the small path from the woods onto the mowed, clear-cut grass area, which left him standing at the southwest corner of the camping area. He was back in his familiar world with a renewed purpose. He stopped and shut his eyes to make sure the actions of the morning would be etched in his memory. Coy's perspective of the world changed this morning as he no longer saw just a man-made world. He was beginning to see the other world.

In some unspecified space deep inside his soul, Coy could not help but believe Growler was misunderstood. And if he was, Coy needed to figure out why his newfound older friend did not try harder to be understood. Why was it so hard for some folks, good and bad alike, to want to be like the rest of the flock? Coy thought about how some who lived with outside mysterious purposes were often labeled weird or a lone seagull looking and flying faster than the rest of the flock and finding his life and food outside the fray with peace and inner contentment. Coy was hoping for peace and inner contentment.

Coy was maturing into the young man stage of life, where young adults began to realize life was really an unknown and everything somehow became unknowable. He was feeling hunger pain, and his stomach was making noises. He knew it was time for some breakfast. Consequently, he decided to make his way back to Little Mora. However, his mind was filled with many thoughts about why any of us were born and when did we find out why and for what? He knew it was for more than to eat and survive or just to stay alive as long as we possibly could, and he could only guess it was for some better reason.

Coy had made a vow to himself three months earlier on his twelfth birthday. He wanted to be different. He wanted to be the person that lives behind his golden-brown eyes. He wanted to know life and not just see life. He was finding out it sure felt like life was a struggle, and nothing seemed to be a game anymore. Mindless and unthinking activities were no longer as fun as they used to be. He knew having fun would have to be part of his life. However, he did not know where or when.

While carefully listening to sermons at church services, participating in church fellowship time, after baseball practice with the other parents, or family get-togethers, Coy slowly began deciphering that boredom, fear, and anger were the reasons life was so short-lived.

Everything seemed like a mystery. "Oh well," he spoke out loud with a sigh as he thought about the price of being misunderstood. "They can call you devil, or they call you something else." He did not care what people called or thought of him. Coy's self-awareness was one of his personality strengths, and he was beginning to understand people had a hard time appreciating other people's strengths.

The pain and reality of being a Missouri Synod Lutheran was settling in. He was right in the middle of confirmation classes at church. He was so glad that they were done for the summer. "Thank God," he murmured.

He did not understand. He was struggling at trying to figure out how anyone could understand what this being confirmed or affirmed was all about. *Why are we forced to answer a list of religious questions when we never asked or wanted to ask any of those questions?* He felt a mixture of not caring, and not really knowing or wanting to know, all mixed up like a pail of fish guts or something worse. Nevertheless, this whole misunderstanding thing popped up in a conversation a couple weeks before when the pastor teaching the class said this Jesus fellow was the most misunderstood man who ever walked this earth. And in turn, as we walked our walk, we would be misunderstood in life as well.

Coy was walking eastward in the direction of Little Mora. He was directly behind the fish house. Coy's world and life path were changing by the moment, and he realized things were changing every day. He thought about how nice it would be if he would not think so much. However, ironically, he liked thinking, and he hungered for learning, as it made life much more interesting. He found the tree stump by the well pump outside behind the fish house and decided to sit down and catch his breath and, more importantly, catch up on his thinking.

CHAPTER 9

Flashback to Confirmation

Coy sat down on a tree stump. He went into Coy wandering-mind time.

Grandpa was correct. Coy was a daydreaming, thinking young man. Coy's mind flashed back to when he was on the way home one night from confirmation class this past spring. He remembered thinking, *There must be some reason we spend so much time trying to understand this Jesus.* He remembered it had been a great day at school, and especially in his English class. Therefore, during the Jesus discussion at confirmation class, he could not figure out if Jesus was a noun, pronoun, object, or a verb. He just knew there was a good chance Jesus's identity could be all of them.

During confirmation class, his attention deficit was on high in top form. His mind and thoughts were running wild, which was a usual occurrence during classes, lectures, or sermons. Coy would fight within himself during those times of teaching as he tried to constantly evaluate and out-think the teacher or speaker. Sometimes he would later be reminded he did not listen very well during his time of distracted thinking. He thought maybe he was trying too hard to out-think this

Growler mystery before him and not listening for the simple real messages.

Like in confirmation classes, his mind was floating around like a boat floating with no anchor, thinking about questions as ridiculous as "Why do we have to keep de-rocking fields every spring?" His mind jumped into trying to understand how and why rocks kept growing out of the fields after each winter. Every spring, the earth pushed rocks up in the fields, and they all had to go out there and dig those rocks up again and again before the spring planting. He could not understand that, either. Somehow the rock wanted to be in the light and not stuck underground.

CHAPTER 10

The Fish House

Coy returned to the present, and he stood up and looked over at the fish house. He figured it made sense to inspect it and make sure it was ready for the day. Coy thought it would not be that big a deal. He and Growler were the last ones in there the night before cleaning a fish for the morning breakfast or lunch or whenever it worked out best to fry them up.

Coy walked over to the fish house and looked it over thoroughly. The fish house and the cabins were built about the same time using similar materials. The fish house was a miniature version of the cabins, about six by ten feet with a flat low slope tin roof, which really added to the fun of cleaning fish with the cacophony of raindrop noises during rainstorms. The house stood perfectly east/west and when standing and cleaning fish, he faced the lake directly and the small playground, tree swing, and the backs of Cabins 4, 5, and 6. The Cabins blocked the view of the lake.

The view toward the back of the cabins would often instigate conversations while watching the kids and people. One could see the end of Dock 4, which was the longest and most used dock. There always seemed to be a few people at the end of the dock, wetting a line to catch a few more fish to clean. People could fish and catch a fish off any of the docks, but Dock 4 was long enough to just be at the edge of a nice lily pad weed line.

The fish house was completely enclosed with fully screened surrounding windows and a screen door. Coy learned to really appreciate the screened-in enclosure during those later-in-the-evening cleaning sessions, as the buzzing of mosquitoes, fireflies, and what seemed like thousands of other flying insects were stopped dead in their tracks right outside the screened-in fortress.

The fish house was split in half by a wood counter that was the cleaning table, built in the north side, about three-and-a-half feet off the floor. The house comfortably held three or four people. The floor was roughly poured solid concrete with one floor drain right below the fish guts hole in the cleaning table. The floor could be easily washed off and swept clean after a cleaning session. Inside the house, people could look over to the outside world though the surrounding screens. The screens also made it possible to have an audience of family, friends, and for sure a few youngsters, watching while the fish were being cleaned. Most of the time, people surrounded the fish house during cleaning sessions to listen in on the conversation and sometimes arguments going on. The real advantage of the screened shelter was that it provided a barrier from the real world of insects and people not needed to perform the task, which was cleaning fish.

Every subject in the world would be discussed in the fish house. However, often everything ended up being about religion or politics. The subject of Jesus was almost always discussed. However, sometimes the rain was all there was left to talk about.

One Lifetime Is Not Enough!

Coy stepped into the fish house and immediately knew someone had been cleaning fish already this morning. He peeked below the guts hole into the five-gallon pail sitting on the floor below. He was right, a few heads and guts from an early morning catch were in the pail. He thought that was interesting.

Coy thought hard, trying to figure out who in the world could have been in the fish house. Whoever it was, he/she had done a pretty good job cleaning up. Coy stepped out of the house and pumped the water pump situated out the back side of the house. He reentered the house once he had the water flowing, and turned the small faucet connected permanently to an old garden hose and sprayed off the cleaning table and floor. He took the old hand brush hanging on the nail to the left side of the door and brushed off the counter and the cleaning boards. He sprayed down the floor, leaving the guts pail, and made sure all the boards, fish scalers, old knives, and brushes were right where they were to be hung up on the nails in the screen frames. He left the fish house. However, he did know later in the morning when the early fishermen came in around eight or so with their morning catch, they would clean their fish and have a quick breakfast. The fish house would need to be checked again and the guts pail dumped later in the morning. Coy learned it was around ten in morning or so when the official first of the day fish house once-over was the most appropriate time to finish up that chore. Grandpa or Growler usually checked on the fish house. Coy would follow them, as it was fun to see the size of the fish heads and the pile of guts in the pail.

CHAPTER 11

New Life Style

Coy stepped out of the fish house and heard a commotion over by Cabin 4.

Those were the folks who arrived late in the afternoon, whom he was not able to meet. He hadn't yet met them because he was mowing the lawn across the gravel road where the resort stored boats, docks, and a bunch of junk from years and years of collection in a small pole barn. The lawn mowing duty was the distraction that kept him from being with Grandpa at the meet and greet time with the new folks.

The night before, Grandpa mentioned some information about the new arrivals at the fire outside the Little Mora Cabin. He mentioned to Coy they were from Chicago, or somewhere 500 to 600 miles away. A friend or someone in their family heard the fishing was great up here at Lake Esquagamah in Northern Minnesota. This was where they were planning on settling in for two weeks. Grandpa mentioned different family and friends of theirs would be coming and going during the week, but the folks who came in were the "base family" and were good people. He informed Coy the family and friends had been at the resort a few years in a row. He also said there were a few young ladies whom Coy might have a chance with, but Coy did not quite get it at the time. However, because he was understanding Grandpa a little more each day, he kind of got the drift.

Coy enjoyed and looked forward to the meet and greet, even though he had an introverted disposition. Yet, he was disappointed he was not at this one. He always thought his initial impressions and discussions were perfect for prejudging and figuring out the new arrivals. Coy had been at the resort for short time and had attended four meet and greet. Each of them had their own feel and character, but this one had five or more new kids coming to the resort and into his world.

However, his stomach was rumbling and making it clear he was more than a little hungry. Nevertheless, the grumbling would have to wait because it was a perfect time to snoop and check out the newcomers. He knew he needed a whole bunch more time to decipher his early morning investigative work, and thinking about other people and other situations was just what the doctor ordered. The distraction might augment his ruminations. Further, Growler would fry up a couple pieces of bacon and a few fish and leave them in the ice box or on the table. It only would take him a few minutes to do a quick stop by Little Mora anyway and eat them up when he had the chance. Some mornings, Coy would do the cooking and leave the food for Growler, the same way Growler taught him.

Moment by moment, Coy could not help but think he was living more and more with an independence of thoughts and actions. Naturally, he was realizing he did not have to get up and eat when Mom had breakfast ready. He could get up because it was his idea. He did not have to get up and go over to Aunt Louise's house because Mom had to work. She would not let Coy and his sister stay home alone. Coy was realizing distractions caused by others were far less for Coy now. He was one of the boys. He could live, eat, and survive on his own time, in his own way, right along with all the other grown-up folks, or so he thought.

This unregulated lifestyle sometimes meant having to miss or postpone breakfast, or having a late snack back at Little Mora. Sometimes gracious cabin patrons would offer up some leftovers and call Coy over, and he obliged as part of his outgoing desire to be polite. It was a nice way to get to know the folks. He could drink water from the well whenever he wanted and each time he had to prime the pump, he was getting better at priming it and getting the water to flow. Instead of grabbing a clean glass filled with water Mom or Dad handed to him, he had to and could do it on his own. No, none of that—he was on his own. Although, he did miss being looked after occasionally and being under the shield of his mom and dad. Nevertheless, every day his self-reliance was growing, being built up, and strengthened.

However, unhappy thoughts would occasionally pop into his mind. Coy thought often about his grandma and that he would never be able to get up and go see her or listen to her wisdom. He missed both grandmas. He missed hugs and encouraging words from his mom that he often carried throughout each day. He realized now the wisdom from the grandmas and didn't want to miss anything from Mom.

Coy knew if he wanted to explore, he could explore. If he wanted to discover, he would try to discover. If he wanted to talk, he talked. If he wanted to not talk, he did not talk. If he wanted to go fishing, he fished. If he fell or cut himself or pinched his hand in a door, he did not have to cry when he was alone. There was no use crying for himself. The survival duties of life were always present, but he had free will, liberty, and independence. This place was becoming a small glimpse of heaven right here on earth. Heaven, where free will was always present and freedom was more than imagined.

Coy had so much going through his mind. Death, life, meaning, church, fish, Jesus, Growler, and now new people filled him with more thoughts. However, his curiosity was overwhelming, and he hoped there would be something interesting over at Cabin 4.

Coy swallowed, then breathed deeply. He felt a level of integrity. He felt a devotion to himself that he could and would "walk his talk," which was one of those Mom things that kept pounding in his thoughts today and every day. She would tell him to honor himself. "Lying, cheating, deceiving, and manipulating your way to success is not a life, Coy." If he heard it once from her, he heard it a thousand times.

Already this morning, a great deal had happened in Coy's life, and he was quite literally barely out of the woods. He was back in the security of the resort world and only steps back into his real world; again, flashes of advice from his mother etched into his soul came to mind as constant reminders. His temples and thought processes pounded and felt like a fish stunned from a good whack so he could hold on before he filleted.

Mom would be proud, he thought. The good kind of proud. Something did stick! Down deep, Coy knew those thoughts generally only came to him when he was doing something really wrong or really right. Usually, a sweat added to these moments in time but not this morning.

He didn't think he was on an incorrect path, just an unknown one. However, it did bother him he was spying on Growler. He felt he was pushing too hard and trespassing on another. "Trespass" was in The Lord's Prayer, and Coy was confused on what that meant. This morning, he felt a trespass presence.

Coy walked around the fish house and started heading to Cabin 4, but stopped by the tree swing just north of the fish house. Loneliness was sweeping and creeping into his thoughts and stopped him in his tracks. It was a personal lonely people felt from being separated from their normal routine or from their family or friends. Coy stopped himself. He did not want to waste his time with that type of feeling and thoughts. Nevertheless, deep down deep he had a sense of loneliness. He could only speculate that all people were lonely deep down when they were alone, especially during deep thought and spiritual time. Part of the penance of being an introvert was an awareness of alone time without the desire to be with others. However, it was very easy to justify the desire to be alone because of a lack of energy to be gregarious and to be with people.

Coy walked over to the tree swing. He could hear music from a radio, coming from the back window in Cabin 4. The music relieved him from his deep thoughts. He could not make out the song on the radio, but he could hear the melody. The radio was in a perfect location for the occupants of both Cabins 4 and 5 to enjoy. The music provided pleasant background. Cabin 4 and Cabin 5 were situated with their door entrances facing each other, about ten to fifteen feet apart. It worked well when larger groups and families occupied both cabins. It was like having one place, with a little space between. Screen doors on more than powerful springs were slamming all day long. Coy knew there was life, as he heard voices the doors opening and closing.

Coy liked music but really had no skill in the music world. Nevertheless, music had become a very important part of his life. The poetry of the wording and the melodies would always bring him to other worlds or places. Sometimes. he was grown up with a wife and kids; sometimes, he was racing a car at the Indy 500 and winning. Sometimes, he was catching the biggest fish; sometimes he was scoring the go-ahead touchdown or hitting the winning homerun in the bottom of the ninth inning. Sometimes he was falling in love or falling out of love. He had no idea what it was about the music that brought him to places. He appreciated all forms of music, but like Grandpa, he had a liking for country music.

Coming out of the radio this morning was something different. Everyone listened to KKIN, the station coming from the radio tower visible from Pontius Bay, back around the corner of the lake from the resort. KKIN only played country music or as Grandpa would say, they played three types of music—country, western and Paul Harvey. Coy, being a small music buff, knew this morning's music was from the band, The Doors. He liked it and for some reason, "Come on baby light my fire…" was etched in his mind. Even though he could not hear the words, he could hear the music and knew most of the words, and he sang along. Albeit, He sang quietly because he did not like his singing.

CHAPTER 12

Tree Swing

Life is like a swing. When you go one way, you always come back. Coy's youthful exuberance was developing right before his eyes and, more importantly, in his heart and soul. In the past year, he realized that often in his enthusiasm he was too hopeful and confident. Therefore, he decided at this point it might be best to take a quick break and breather to collect his thoughts and ponder his experience of the young day before heading in the direction of Cabin 4. He sat down in the half tire tree swing behind Cabin 5. The break might have been equally physical and mental. He knew he needed a minute.

The latent sense of family habits began to pound into his temples. He spoke under his breath as he sat down in the old tire swing, "Always be a moving kid." Coy knew he should always be very careful to look like he was working hard with an industrious appearance. Therefore, stopping and sitting on a tree swing to catch his breath and gather his thoughts initially felt wrong. He knew better but went with it. Yet, he did not want Grandpa or anyone to think he was lazy or did not care. His time on the swing would have to be short.

Grandpa, like his mother, was a worker and a doer. However, Grandpa did take an afternoon nap or two but during his awake time, Grandpa was always doing, moving, fixing, and thinking, and those were traits Coy wanted to possess. Stopping and resting sometimes felt like an improper response to something-a something he just could not put his finger on.

Coy glanced over to Little Mora Cabin. He could see the front entrance and the north side, as it was directly east and within eyeshot of the fish house and swing area. He looked eastward and across the other side of the two-track road entrance toward the lake and saw the cabin patrons' vehicles parked next to their respective cabins. He looked at the resort entrance road, which ended at the lake and doubled as the public access to the lake. The public access was nothing fancy, but it worked. Coy had already been out in the water helping folks unload their boats. Grandpa told Coy he would likely have to be in the water again, helping them load up the boats. Even the boat landing resembled the rest of the resort: a little beat-up yet functional and often it took extra effort to launch and load boats. Someone would always get wet at the boat landings.

Coy's suspicion was confirmed. Grandpa was doing his chores this morning as usual. Grandpa spent many mornings on the north side of the Little Mora cabin. The roof on the north side hung over about six feet, and the area sheltered under it became a workbench and shelving area providing storage for miscellaneous maintenance items. This was where bait was stored and motors were repaired. Grandpa built a launching pad to mount the small Johnson, Evinrude, Mercury, and a couple beat-up Montgomery Ward outboard motors where he could work on them. Fifty-five-gallon drums were set up under the cover on the sides of the work bench. He could run the motors to make sure his repairs were okeydokey before carrying them down to the dock and remounting them on the boats. It was a challenge stepping into a boat with a motor in. Mounting them on the red aluminum resort-owned and resort-named boats labeled Little Mora's helpers would only be done after Grandpa was sure the motor was ready. Grandma had painted the names on both sides of the boats. Grandpa told Coy he never really liked the name, but he would not even think about changing the name or painting on new names, as they always reminded him of Grandma. It reminded Coy that Grandpa and Grandma were also husband and wife and when one of them was taken to heaven, life still moved on and the little things helped carry the strain.

Grandma once told Coy, "You know, when we were younger and trying to impress people and/or the world, we used to spend hours and hours of our time cleaning up the house. We would make sure the windows did not have any kid's fingerprints on them. But now when the grandkids come around about once or twice a month, we do not clean up those fingerprints on the windows anymore." When Coy heard the story at the time, he did not understand; now he did.

The fading of the names painted on the sides of the resort boats was evident. Coy could see Grandpa had a little different look and response when someone would ask about the name and question if they would ever be repainted or touched up. Grandpa would not respond. Memories faded slowly enough but sometimes not fast enough and if the good ones could be prolonged, it was often wise to just do it without a need to explain.

Grandpa was one arm deep into one of the Evinrude motors. It was one of the motors where the carburetor would gum up from the gas and the choke would jam. It always took a little true elbow grease to work on the motors. He always seemed to have the knowledge, and he would get the motors running and working again and again. Occasionally, he would swing over his now missing right arm at the joint to hold the other side of a tight nut and bolt. His mind would forget his arm was not there, but his body said, "No! I am not here anymore and never will be again!"

Those were just the thoughts Coy needed to refresh. He understood why Grandpa did not want to repaint the boats.

CHAPTER 13

Hilding

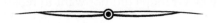

Coy's time on the swing was only a few minutes and his mind did not take any time off. There were many times during the day when Coy's thoughts wanted him to be on that swing.

The familiar sound of a vehicle on the gravel road was enough of a distraction to catch Coy's attention while he started his trek back to Little Mora world. It was Hilding in his '61 Chevy step-side pickup, rolling down the hill and passing the resort entrance on his way to his small farmstead about a mile down the road. Hilding and Grandpa were friends. He often stopped by to chew the fat. Hilding stopped by to chew the fat a couple of days before.

Coy had liked Hilding right away and could tell he was not the judgmental type. He also had a cool truck. Hilding did not take the time to fake anything. He would come down to the resort or stop by on his way through to his place and drop off fresh eggs, bacon, or some other necessities for Grandpa. Sometimes, he would ask for a hand or a little help haying or field de-rocking or anything. Grandpa would always go and help. Coy wanted to be like that. Growler went along occasionally. Coy went when he could or when Grandpa needed help and, more importantly, needed help understanding Hilding. Hilding spoke with a half-Norwegian, half-German broken type of English. He rolled his words. Coy thought it was real fun listening to him. Grandpa would laugh. The laughter did not make Hilding feel bad. He laughed his hearty and fun-loving laugh along. Laughing and living together, not a bad thing after all. Hilding and Grandpa had a nice relationship.

Hilding's English was so broken up; the slurred-out English was like a whole new language. It really was exhausting trying to figure out what he was trying to convey. Often, people would give the obligatory "yes" nod. It became a game between Grandpa and Coy to figure out what Hilding said or directed. Sometimes, they both knew what Hilding said and would look at each other with an instinctive shrug of their shoulders and a sigh, they "spoke" that they both understood Hilding. He would get more and more frustrated even though he laughed along. Grandpa, Growler, and Coy would smile at each other but not too much so as not to hurt Hilding's feelings. But it was funny. Growler never said anything out loud when around Hilding, but it seemed he was a step or two ahead of Grandpa and Coy as if he knew what Hilding was saying. Growler always seemed to have almost every situation figured out.

CHAPTER 14

The Road Less Traveled

The meet and greet trek to Cabin 4 would have to wait. Coy was starvation and decided to return to Little Mora. He stepped into the cabin and was all alone. He sat down at the table and ate breakfast. Coy took two leftover fried sunfish Growler had left on the table and made a couple pieces of toast. He ate it all up as though it was his last meal. He washed down his breakfast with orange nectar drink, which was always made fresh and available in the ice box. Coy liked calling it the ice box even though it looked like a refrigerator.

Coy took his first couple of bites and heard a vehicle heading down the gravel road and thought it must be Hilding. He thought about the road and could not help but think the gravel road was the exit from this world back to his old world, or maybe a far-off new world. Coy usually thought in opposites for some reason, and the gravel road could be an exit or an entrance, depending upon a particular point of view.

The road was approximately eight miles of gravel road off Minnesota State Highway 169, literally an old gravel road in the middle of nowhere. The entire road, approximately twenty miles in total length, went all the way around Lake Esquagamah and ended up coming around to an east/west intersection exactly two miles due north of the highway. The road fed the world to cabins, three resorts, and several homesteads.

As far as townships, the closest was a good fifteen miles or so west and seven miles east of the Robinson Corner exit, which was the right turn off State Highway 169. The Robinsons owned and ran a small repair shop on the corner off 169; thus, the reason it was called Robinson Corner. The road was very close to being considered a minimum maintenance gravel road. The road did not go more than 150 feet without a turn or well-worn slow-down bumps and low spots filled with water and mud. Right off the highway, there were farmers' fields for the first two miles up to the intersection. Grandpa knew all the history, all the farmers, all the good-looking wives, kids, religions, occupations, and lifestyles of all the folks who owned or had any connection with the land all the way from the highway to the resort and around the lake.

During the evening fires, Grandpa would make conversation about all the people and the histories. Coy found it hard to listen sometimes, but he did listen carefully and found it all very interesting. Besides, he just enjoyed hearing Grandpa talk.

Grandpa and Coy went to town once, and Coy just listened. He was amazed by Grandpa's memory. Besides the internal quiet time, riding in the truck gave him time while Grandpa was talking and babbling on about so and so, and so-and-so, and he would count the fence posts, while thinking about how much work it must have been to connect all that beat-up barbed wire fencing.

There were three decrepit bridges on the road between the highway and the resort. The first was a dry swamp area that would flood in the spring. The road would wash away sometimes since there was not a big enough bridge built over the road. The second bridge was over the Mississippi River. The river was only twenty feet wide there and maybe only three or four feet deep. The river's formation was only eighty to ninety miles away up north by Itasca, which was where the great Mississippi River started. This bridge had the most beef to it. The third bridge was over Jordan Creek. This was the creek that fed Lake Esquagamah to the north and was more or less a tributary feeding off the Mississippi. There was a small creek called Jordan Brook, which came off the south end of the lake and not too far from the resort. There wasn't a bridge over Jordan Brook, just a culver built in below the gravel road. Some of the best fishing was near the creek and brook inlets and outlets. Beautiful-sized sunfish, nice-sized northern fish walleyes, bass, and, of course, bullheads could be caught by the dozens each day.

It was not easy to spot the resort gravel road off Highway 169. It was not marked other than the red-sided small Robinson building at the corner. Someone not paying close attention would drive right by as the road became hilly near the lake. In fact, the hill next to the resort was always a challenge- both going up and down. Grandpa once told Coy that way in the past, the Model T's had to go up the hill backwards. The transmission in the Model T's just did not have the strength to pull the hill. "Folks always found a way to make it work, and sometimes going backwards works better than going forwards," Grandpa would say.

Coy finished up eating. There was always a pail of water sitting next to the sink under the window of the south wall of the cabin. Coy took the scoop from the hook on the wall on the right side of the window, dipped it in the water, and put some in the sink. He splashed in some dishwashing soap and cleaned up his plate and cup and dried them with a towel. He put the plate on the shelf above the ice box and hung the cup above the small sink.

It was now back to reality for Coy. He stepped out of the cabin and immediately looked around to check on Grandpa as he walked around to the north side of the cabin. He looked over to the east and caught sight of the two-holer, about fifty feet behind Little Mora. He immediately realized it was time for a little backside movement. He headed to the two-holer. It was pretty amazing to him that this was the early '70s, and his grandpa was the only person he knew who was born in the 1800s and still lived in a world with no indoor bathroom or plumbing. No big deal to Coy, but it was fun to see how the new city folk vacationers handled the two-holer, especially the girls.

Grandpa caught a glimpse of Coy. They made a polite unspoken gesture to each other and went about their business. One thing for sure though, Coy did not like going with someone to the two-holer. One at a time is enough for him, even for number two.

CHAPTER 15

Pojken, He talks!

Coy was becoming more and more accustomed to his new existence and environment daily. A few days later and mid-morning, Coy and Growler were off doing a few chores. Grandpa finished his work on one of the Mercury seven-and-a-half motors by fixing the shifter shaft and the arm on the left side of the motor, which had become stripped from wear caused by age and hurried shifting. It had been a problem for a while. However, with ingenuity and an innate engineering mind (which apparently all good farmers seemed to possess), he once again was able to get whatever he was working on to work again.

The night before, right before dark and early dusk, a couple fellows from Cabin 2 came to the campfire outside the Little Mora Cabin with the seven-and-a-half Mercury. They were telling the story of what happened and making Grandpa aware of a problem. Grandpa was sitting in a chair, stoking the fire. They told him the motor on their Cabin 2 boat was not working right. They went on to tell the story of how they had to go all the way across the lake in reverse when it was starting to get dark, and they were nervous but laughing while telling him the story. They were not mad or upset as they took the incident in stride and marked it up as a fun lake story takeaway. After all, they were on vacation and there to recreate. Besides, they did catch a twelve-pound northern fish and four nice-sized walleyes. They still had a fishy stench of accomplishment with happy smirks on their face.

Grandpa immediately knew what the issue was and applauded them for their catch. He apologized to them for their inconvenience. He then told the two gentlemen to take the five-and-a-half Mercury off the boat on Dock 1, knowing they would want to go out in the morning. Grandpa's boat was docked on Dock 1 and the five-and-a-half was his personal motor. He was always willing to give it up to accommodate the patrons. Coy knew Grandpa would give up his left arm if he had to help others. This was definitely a personality trait that was very enduring to Coy, and one he wanted.

Coy and Growler had a couple armfuls of firewood, and now joined them at the fire pit, and the guys told them the story also. They all laughed.

Grandpa smiled but was not laughing as much. He stood up and walked over the north side of the cabin.

"Hey, guys. Grab the motor and bring it over here." Grandpa spoke loudly from the side of the cabin to Coy and Growler. Both came to attention. Growler immediately stepped over and grabbed the motor from the fellows. When Grandpa spoke up, everyone knew he was the leader and something must need to be done. Coy was pleased to be called out as one of the guys. "Come over here, guys, and help me put the seven-and-a-half on the rack so we can take a look." Grandpa pointed to the rack with his left arm. Growler put the motor on the rack and tightened up the wing nuts to hold it in place.

"Give those boys a hand if they need it, and help them get the five-and-a-half off my boat." Grandpa was speaking but looking at the motor. He was deep in thought on how to get it fixed up.

"Will do," Coy answered for them. Growler and Coy turned back to the boys and fire pit.

One of them spoke up and said, "No problem. We can take care of grabbing the motor." Coy was a bit relieved.

"We will go get the motor right now before it gets too dark. Would that be okay?" one of the fellows asked loudly while looking over at Grandpa.

Grandpa lifted his head, turned, and responded, "Of course, be careful."

Then the other fellow answered, "Thank you very much. You are a fine man. Don't let anyone tell you different."

Grandpa laughed a bit and so did they as they started walking to Dock 1.

Grandpa looked their way for a couple of seconds and had a droll smile on his face. He turned and looked over to Growler and Coy with a more authoritative look and said, "This shouldn't take me very long. I will have to get at it first thing in the morning." Coy and Growler looked at each other. "Stoke the fire, boys," Grandpa said.

The next morning, all three of them got up and went about doing some chores. Grandpa immediately went over and started working on the motor.

They gathered together around 7 o'clock and stepped into the cabin for breakfast.

"Boys, I think I got it fixed up and after we eat, let's get it down to my boat and why don't you two take it out for a spin? If it runs okay, stay out and pick up a few for lunch," Grandpa said, starting the conversation.

Coy's chest was ready to burst. Coy looked over at Growler who had a different look in his face. Coy did not think much of it right then because Growler always had some kind of different look, but this look was new to Coy.

After they cleaned up the breakfast dishes and put things away, all three of them stepped out of the cabin and made their way to the north side of the cabin where the motor was still mounted in the repair area. That was when it occurred to Coy that Grandpa was a pretty shrewd operator. He wanted them to carry the motor down to the lake, walk out onto the dock, step into the boat with the motor, step over the seats of the small fourteen-foot Lund boat, drop the motor in its place, and tighten the wing-nut clamps that held the motor to the boat.

Coy was the first to reach the motor. It was perched and attached on a makeshift support system that looked like the back of a boat attached to the north outside wall of the cabin and under the overhang. Coy loosened up the wing nuts and grabbed ahold of the motor to make sure it was loose, and started to lift it up to get ready to head down to the dock.

"Holy cow!" Coy meekly shouted.

Grandpa and Growler were now right behind him and watched the action before them. "What is it, Pojken?" Grandpa said as he looked on.

Coy never really liked the Pojken name. Grandma told him it was an endearing way to say young boy in Swedish or Norwegian. He thought Grandpa called him Pojken to make sure that he remains a young boy or something. It was okay when he was younger, but now Coy felt he was well on his way to manhood. Grandpa knew exactly what he was saying, though. The motor was heavy, and Coy could not budge the motor off its perch, let alone handle it enough to carry it down to the dock.

Coy stepped back, looked at his seventy-eight-year-old, one-armed grandfather, and blurted, "How did you get this up here?"

Just as Grandpa expected no sympathy for only having one arm, in turn he had no sympathy for an open weakness exposed from his young grandson. He simply responded, "I can handle it." Another lesson learned.

Growler stepped forward, grabbed ahold of the motor, and pulled it off its perch. He lifted it up, swung it down and held it on his right side like a suitcase. He immediately started walking to Dock 1. Grandpa walked right behind him, and Coy, like a wet little puppy, followed them both. "Oh, well," Coy mumbled.

Coy was back in action by the time they reached the dock. "Can I help you, Growler?" He knew he would not get a verbal response, but he innately knew that with a sly look from this old man, a response would be shown. Either that or Grandpa would answer and help Coy understand. Coy by now never expected any response other than a grunt, and a grunt-like growl was what he received from Growler. Coy took that as a "yes." He maneuvered around Grandpa and asked what he could do.

Grandpa said, "Hold the boat, Pojken, with as much as you got, tight to the dock, so he can step in the boat without it tipping too much, and give the boat some balance."

This time it did not bother Coy that Grandpa called him Pojken. The instruction was given and received and Coy jumped into attention. He was not going to mess this one up, and he held the boat with all he had and as tight as he could muster. Growler stepped in the boat off the dock, and the boat immediately rocked heavily to the point of almost taking in water. However, he caught his balance and leveled off the boat by moving to the center of the seat top he was standing on. He stepped down off the middle seat and stepped on the bottom of the boat in front of the back seat and sat down. He then maneuvered the motor around and to the back of the boat and dropped the motor down carefully in its place, exactly where it belonged. Coy watched and could not help but think at that moment how strong this man was, and he wished he would become just as strong.

Growler stepped back, moved up a few seats to the front area of the boat, and looked up at Grandpa for approval. He received a nod and responded with a grunt. Coy immediately jumped in the boat to the back next to the motor and looked up at Grandpa. He understood the look and hooked up the gas line from the small can he had filled with gas earlier, sitting between the last seat and the back of the boat on the bottom of the boat. Coy attached the gas line to the motor and pumped the squeeze ball in the line to prime the motor. He checked to make sure the motor was tightly attached, and confirmed Growler did his job. Coy unlatched the motor lock, so it would move down to proper position in the water, but not all the way down yet because Coy knew the water was shallow near the dock.

Coy primed the carburetor by squeezing the prime ball in the fuel line again and pushed the choke button twice as Grandpa had instructed and showed him in the past. He made sure the motor was in neutral and pulled the cord. It started right up. While all this was happening, Grandpa untied the boat from the dock. Coy looked up and, as usual, was amazed at Grandpa's natural aptitude to know the next move. It was just like playing cards with him. Coy was always amazed by how Grandpa seemed to know the card Coy was going to discard.

Growler took out one of the oars and used it to push away from the dock and out to deeper water while guiding the boat, helping it point forward and away from the dock. Coy lowered the motor down one more click and reached to the right side of the motor and pulled the shifter lever to F – for forward. Coy confirmed that Grandpa reattached the lever correctly and it appeared to be working. Coy gently twisted the throttle and guided the boat out into the main body of water. He could not tell if his feelings were happiness or amazement.

They moved away from the dock area and out of earshot from the shoreline. Coy had not grabbed a handful of throttle. Grandpa had taught him and even scolded him a few times to take it easy around the docks and resort. "Be a gentleman around the resort and not an idiotic racer or something. You will have plenty of time to race in your life. Hold off a bit more." Coy remembered Grandpa reciting this to him a few days before when they went out for a quick spin.

Coy was looking back at the motor with some mild amazement that Grandpa was able to fix another motor and/or figured out another problem once again, when an unrecognizable human voice from out of nowhere spoke up.

"How does it work?"

The surprise of the spoken word caused Coy to spin his head around to figure out what just happened and to figure out where the question came from. This voice and sound were extremely intelligent, authoritative, soft, and caring all in one. Coy had never heard that type of voice or sound before.

"Well, how does it work?" came again, aimed in Coy's direction.

Coy turned around completely and was now looking right at Growler. He now knew the words came from his direction. Coy took a deep breath and looked at this new man sitting six feet in front of him in this small fishing boat.

"Did you hear something? Someone asked me how it works." He spoke in the direction of Growler.

"The shifting apparatus and gear connection, son," came directly from what was once Growler's non-speaking mouth. "How does it work?"

Coy had been at the resort for a couple of weeks and covertly followed Growler around. He had been out on the lake and fished with Grandpa and Growler many hours. He had been in the fish house many hours and helped clean fish at night with Grandpa and Growler. He played at least a hundred card games with Growler and not once did he see or hear this man speak. Coy had concluded he could not speak or communicate with words but with grunts and growls. Coy had determined the name Growler was given with fitting recognition.

"Are you speaking? I mean are you talking to me?" Coy responded with utter bewilderment.

"Yes, of course. Who else? We are alone here, son." This new man now looked right through and penetrated the space behind Coy's eyes and mind and waited for his response.

"Why, why have you not spoken before?" Coy spat out with some trepidation.

"Many reasons but, most importantly, there really wasn't anyone interesting enough to talk with," the old man eloquently responded. "Besides, I like you. You have the face of a dreamer. You remind me of myself at twelve, Coy."

"I know your name is not Growler. What is your real name? There doesn't seem to be anyone who can tell me, and no one seems to know." Coy could barely stop his mouth from running on with lively interest.

There was a moment of hesitation. It was a beautiful, partly cloudy, seventy-five-degree day and the rays of sunlight were hidden behind a cloud and had not reached Coy, yet he was sweating with anticipation.

"I will give you my history and name in time. You can call me an enigma for now," this new gentleman responded with what seemed like a glimpse of newfound joy.

Coy, of course, had no idea what that was supposed to mean or what that was all about. He always thought people proudly gave their names when asked. This fellow's answer seemed a little absurd. Most people wanted to tell their story and spit it out. So much so, most of the time in conversations with others, Coy would find himself daydreaming as people talked and talked about themselves. Coy thought everyone else seemed to think the rest of the world should and would be more interested in them than they deserved. He was still stunned by what had just happened. He remembered what they were in the boat for in the first place, which was to check out the motor to make sure it all worked okay and possibly go and catch a couple of fish.

"Thanks for grabbing some worms in the ice box before we came out here. I see them in your shirt pocket," Coy stuttered.

The new gentleman brought it right back to the beginning. "Well, how does it work?"

"How does what work?" Coy responded.

"The motor."

"Oh yeah, the motor... well, let's see."

Coy turned the handle and grabbed a handful of throttle. All was well. He looked at Growler and spoke loudly over the motor and boat noise. "It works great!"

Coy knew even a small boat with a seven-and-a-half Mercury would go about twelve miles an hour and was fast enough in the small Lund boat they were in. For a moment, he thought about swinging the motor a hard turn so he would be able to throw out someone sitting in the front of the boat if they were not ready. He was tempted to do it this morning. He didn't know this stranger sitting six feet from him in the front of the boat. However, his curiosity was on high alert and his forbearance came back.

Coy returned to his happy thoughts and realized it was about nine o'clock in the morning and was a pretty decent time of the day; it was right before the heat of the day, and the morning freshness wasn't totally burned away. He liked this time of day because the early morning chores were generally completed, and it was not at the hot point of the day. The whole resort still had that breakfast fresh bacon smell, and he loved bacon.

Coy's mind swam right to the point where he was in the middle of an obsession. The same obsession that had him watching this man closely for answers in the past couple of weeks. He had followed him. He had played cards and cleaned fish with him. They had walked the resort together. They had split and carried wood together. Coy even tried out the two-holer with him. He thought all of that must have been for outward appearances. His goal was for his investigation to provide a chance to learn the inside part of this man. He desired dearly to not judge anyone and especially not just outward appearances. He desired to find the inward appearance. Coy knew the outward appearance was like the skin of a tomato: very thin yet strong enough to protect the softer inners or so he thought more and more each day, the heart and soul.

Coy was close to being stonewalled by this man's outward appearance, and he was ready to accept him as the world did. The inner heart and soul might be something people would never be able to see or even imagine unless they cut them open like cleaning a big bluegill. And even then, they might end up in a five-gallon pail on the floor below the hole in the cleaning table in a fish house. Coy felt there was so much more to Growler and had no idea why he had a desire to know this man. His discovery and realization of the mystery was obviously at a turning point. Outward appearances were so easy. The depths of the heart and soul took a lot more digging. He had no idea what to expect or why he even wanted to expect something more.

"Hey, that is enough," the older gentleman yelled above the sound of the motor and the splashing water on the side of the boat. Coy, falling from his quick daydream, responded immediately by slowing the boat down.

"Your grandfather is an amazing person, young man."

"You can call me Coy."

"I understand, young man; a name is important, is it not?" the mystery man responded.

Coy's meek response was, "Ya." He spoke with his spontaneous shyness that was his usual way with people he didn't know. He also hunched and bunched his shoulders with simplicity and accompanied his words with a smile. He didn't know it but when he responded this way, it lightened his face and took the edge off any youthful roughness.

"I have been watching and following you, and I have like a million questions for you," the shy young man uttered.

"I understand, but let me start with some questions for you first." The gentleman declared.

"What questions could you possibly have for me? Please let me ask the first question?" Coy said with a bit more confidence.

"All right, I will let you have the first play," the seasoned veteran responded.

CHAPTER 16

The First Play

"Why? Why have you not said a word the entire time I have been here? In fact, I asked Grandpa and others, and no one could tell me if they ever heard you speak a word," the inquisitive young man said.

"You are the first person I have spoken with in a very long time. I have been living a life of obscurity within the life chosen for me. I have been assigned to live with a shroud from the world and forthrightly from others and myself for some time now." The old man spoke clearly and with conviction yet with a sad undertone.

Coy did not and couldn't possibly understand.

"Okay, but why? Why are you speaking to me now?" Coy responded, not really hearing what the conversation was about or where it was heading.

"Because I like you, and I desire a conveyance. You appear to be the vehicle that will make sure I have history and future. My hope is that my life and my story are not wiped out forever. I have been searching for a person like you who lives with purpose and someone who cares. You fit the bill perfectly, young man. Even though you are a mere twelve years old, you are perfect, and that is the age my story began," Growler said with purpose, and paused for reflection.

"Now my turn, young man. Why did you follow me up the hill to the white building a few days back, and what did you see and/or hear?" Growler asked more directly, while looking at Coy.

"Well..." Coy paused, as he was taken aback, and sweat started to well up under his Twins baseball cap. "Um, I needed to see what you were doing and somehow try to find out something about you. You are pretty perfectly interesting to me, also."

Even though the young man put it out there, he began to realize he might not be as wise as he had thought. Now with certainty, he realized his secret detective work was not good either.

"Well, then." Growler paused for what Coy thought was just short of an eternity. The words were thrown out there while the older man was looking away and at the lake's western shoreline. Then he broke from his deliberate and timely pause. "Let's wet a line and pick up a few for lunch."

"Okay," Coy mumbled. It was not a mumble of frustration but of relief the conversation was going somewhere else. The distraction of fishing always worked. Coy enjoyed fishing with others, especially with Grandpa. It was an opportunity to talk, listen, and try hard to get to know Grandpa better. Often, he would jump out of the boat onto the dock after they went fishing, mad at himself, realizing he did most of the talking, and it was Grandpa who did most of the listening. Since he was aware of what might happen, he wanted to make sure he asked the right questions and maybe try to listen more than talk this time.

"I hope you understand I was not trying to do anything wrong when I followed you. No, I did not hear or see much, either. Ya, let's catch a couple," Coy said.

"Sounds good to me, Coy, and how about we wet a few lines over in Jordan's Bay in the morning about this time? I thoroughly enjoy Sunday morning fishing time over in the bay. And as you may know, they hit pretty solid over there when we find the undercurrent spot where the cooler water of the river flows though the lake," Growler continued.

Another amazing piece to the puzzle, Coy thought. But more a piece of off-blue in the blue background sky part of a puzzle. It was always tough to finish that part of any puzzle. Coy pondered quietly. *This man pays attention and is not just floating in a boat through life.*

"That sounds great Grow..." Coy stumbled with the Growler name, as he knew it was more than a nickname and could be a title. "... ler. Oh, I am so sorry, but what is your real name?" He spoke confidently and formally, but with trepidation. He was afraid, which came from the anticipation of entering an important, worthwhile task. Coy remembered his Sunday school teacher telling him some fear was good fear.

"Good question," was all that came back Coy's direction.

The back and forth ended. Coy found a spot neatly tucked in behind a lily pad garden with an opening about the size of four boats, and water depth of about four feet and thirty feet off the west shoreline. He stopped the slow troll they were moving in the Little Mora signature boat. The older gentleman dropped the front anchor. They prepared for a quick killing.

The Little Mora signature boat was like all the resort boats; it two oars, one anchor mounted on the front of the boat, and another loose anchor in the back sitting between the back seat and the motor. There was one gas can, which was checked and filled daily. Each boat had two old eight-foot-long cane fishing poles stuffed neatly on the left side under the oar holders. Most people did not use the cane poles, but they were used regularly as backups when folks had to go out and check things out on the lake or take a late afternoon cruise with a grandma or the few lady folks who did not like going out on the water very much. Fishing with the backup cane poles could be done when desired. The cane poles still worked well. Grandpa's Little Mora signature boat had many little extras, like a holder for the pole near the back right side of the boat, which enabled a one-armed man to fish with more ease.

Coy could not keep his eyes off Growler. He looked intently at his neatly groomed, combed straight back hair, which was at least fifty percent gray and Coy thought it to be earned gray and not a natural gray. His eyes had depth with wrinkles and dark circles around and under them, which appeared to have been earned. Coy saw a different soul in front of him.

Without a flinch, the old man carefully removed two cane poles from their hidden position and handed one to Coy. He took the small Styrofoam container of delicious worms out of his shirt pocket. Coy had dug up worms earlier that day, filled ten containers, and put them in the small cooler on the north side of Little Mora. Patrons would leave a note in the small journal hung up on the side of the cabin under the overhang when they came and grabbed a container. The cost would be added to the total bill when their accounts were closed at the end of their stay. The old man dug into the container and laid a worm on the bench between them and went about baiting the hook attached to the line from the cane pole he was planning on using. The movement of Growler's hands when he played cards, cleaned fish, or anything Coy had seen him do was steady, sure, and effortless. Coy noticed all the other older folks in his life had shaky dispositions, but not this older gentleman.

Growler looked at Coy and talked for well over twenty minutes, which felt like a few seconds to Coy. He gave a complete and thorough description of everything he and Coy had done since Coy showed up at the resort. Coy was amazed and overwhelmed. He had never been around anyone who was so aware and attentive to details. The details included the exact number of fish they had cleaned together, descriptions of each cribbage game, and who won and why. Each vignette enthralled Coy with worry and passion. He wanted to be like this old man. He had never been around or aware of anyone who was so observant and aware of life around themselves.

When Growler stopped talking, they silently went about their business, and in their short time of fishing caught seven beautiful blue gill sunfish the size of a big man's hand. That was the measurement that counted for Grandpa, so it worked for them. Coy caught two, and the man now newborn in Coy's eyes caught five. It did not matter how many each person caught. The count that mattered when the boats came back to the dock after fishing was the boat totals. The adults counted the boat totals, and all the people thirteen and under wanted to take the most credit. Coy started to like the total boat count practice, as he did not have the patience of his older friends. He could not stop daydreaming while fishing. Fishing did take practiced patience.

Without even having to say a word, the young man and the older man both put the poles back in their storage spots in the boat. Growler pulled up the anchor, and they sat there for a few minutes and floated around with the waves and listened to the world. A couple of loons were wailing to each other, communicating their eerie, haunting, and beautiful sound across the bay to the main body of water of the lake. Coy could not help but think how distinctive and gorgeous loons were.

Even though it would only take a couple of minutes to get back to Dock 1, each of them knew they needed more time and required more communication.

"You can call me Growler, son." The older gentleman broke the silence and disturbed the place where Coy was at in minded spirit. It was almost like the old man did it on purpose to make sure Coy did not read too much into their new relationship too quickly.

"We'd better get back. Grandpa might be worried we broke down or something, and, besides, I cannot wait to tell him you do talk. We have so much to talk about now."

"No, no... I will not talk with people. It is the cross I have to bear to protect the innocent," Growler responded.

"What do you mean?" Coy bluntly replied.

"Just like your grandfather's lost arm, this is a part of me that cannot be again. We all have handicaps. I will speak only to you, young man. In time I will share with you my history, and I will call it my dilemma or, worse, my cross to bear. A real thorn in my side. However, we do not have time now." Growler stopped to reflect, then continued.

"One of the reasons I really enjoy and appreciate your grandfather and one reason my life landed here is that he and I enjoy an unspoken bond, and to me a virtue, so to speak. I will share this one tidbit with you this morning, young man. Great men have little sympathy for those who blame their plight or poor fortune on handicap. It could be either physical or environmental. Your grandfather's is physical and mine is environmental. You most likely will not understand this philosophy or thought processes right now, Coy," Growler finished abruptly.

Coy responded with a slight growling smile at the mention of his name spoken at the end of those thoughts.

"Touché, just checking to see if you heard me." Growler had heard the growl.

"Two what?" Coy replied immediately.

Growler pushed forward and started to speak with clear diction and dignity. "Milton's blindness, Beethoven's deafness, Lincoln's poverty, Roosevelt's polio, Helen Keller's lack of hearing and seeing, Tchaikovsky's tragic marriage, Isaac Hayes' upsetting early years of poverty. Remember John Bunyan writing *Pilgrim's Progress* while in prison, Charles Dickens pasting labels on blacking pots, Robert Burns and Ulysses S. Grant fighting alcoholism, and Benjamin Franklin dropping out of school when he was only ten, and then we could go on and talk about Paul..."

Growler sensed and he was correct that he undoubtedly lost his audience, even though he was ready to give a bigger and broader list. He had recognized years before, through years of self-learning, that genuine communication happens when there is two-way transmission. Besides, he thought teasing and whetting the appetite of his young friend should really be the basis of this new beginning.

"Well, anyway, I do know I can't give out years of learning and living in one short sitting, son, so let's leave our time of talking together with this... This so carries me through the nights, and through the harassment of life, Coy... No person ever had a defect that was not really a potential benefit rather than an adversity. My hope lies with that. Please understand and remember, young man, sometimes the cards fall differently than desired." Growler abruptly stopped talking.

By the time all that came out, Coy felt like he must have dropped out of school at ten or something as he had no idea what just happened or what was communicated in the last few minutes of his life.

Coy pulled the rope, started the motor, and put it in gear. They headed back to Dock 1. When they were a hundred yards or so from the resort, the noise and ambiance of the resort was ever- present. Life was abounding. People were swimming and taking baths near the shore. A few kids were fishing off Dock 7, doors were being slammed, kids were running around, and the twenty-something girls were sunbathing. Coy did catch one of the attractive middle-aged women with dark hair leaning back in her lawn chair, reading a book and for a moment, he missed his mom.

Safety first, Coy thought. as they worked together and slowly moved the boat into docking position at Dock 1. Growler grabbed the dock and with precision and ease tied the boat safely and securely to the dock. They worked together like a well-oiled machine. Nothing had to be said as the parts just did their part.

"I'll clean the fish, Growler. Is that okay?" Just a look and murmur came back as a response.

It was back to the old reality and back to the mystery for Coy. "Inch by inch, life's a cinch," would be the advice Coy knew would come from his mother at this moment.

It takes an enormous amount of internal self-assurance to begin with the spirit of adventure, discovery, and creativity. Some will add the courage it takes to realize and accept the life process that takes time. Coy felt the adventure waiting, but he had just jumped or had been pushed into the deep end of the pool. He hoped being in the deep end of the pool pushed the adventure forward, and discovery, creativity, and courage would surface. He was overwhelmed with the emotions of what had just happened in his life.

Coy's spirit was filled. He gave a welcome, winsome smile in response to Growler as they docked the boat. He stepped out of the back of the boat as Growler held the boat for balance. Coy in turn held the boat tightly to the dock as Growler stepped out of the boat onto the dock. They worked together very efficiently. Coy reflectively knew he would have to watch every step he took, watch every word he spoke, and every form of communication and action.

Coy turned and looked out and across the calm water of Lake Esquagamah for some silent guidance. He then turned around and walked to the shore on the creaky old dock. The jump onto the shore broke the silence. He grabbed the five-gallon pail sitting near the end of the dock, which Grandpa must have set there knowing they would be bringing in lunch. Coy turned around, sidestepped Growler, and walked back to the boat on the dock and had a feeling he was walking the plank. He jumped back into the boat and put the seven wonders into the pail. Coy then headed to the fish house. Growler had stepped off the dock onto the shoreline in silence and began his walk back to Little Mora. The triumph of communication once again entered his immediate environment. Everything said something about life.

CHAPTER 17

The Resort Was Humming

The resort had that late morning-early afternoon familiar hum and buzz. Coy remembered it was Saturday and from mid-May on, the resort occupancy ballooned on the weekends. There were now additional campers staying in the west side campsite area beyond Cabin 7, and families set up their pop-up campers and large family tents. The clearing for the campsite part of the resort was a good area for camping as the land elevation there was on higher ground compared to the marshy area near the cabins and around Little Mora.

Coy began his trek to the fish house and was walking along the shoreline near the water access ramp area. He could see the camping area and signs of life everywhere.

Most of the lake resort property sat low in elevation. The south bay and the natural half crescent moon bay shoreline appeared to make this land an absolute ideal location for a resort. However, the land wasn't quite as cooperative. Chelsea Brook was actually an overflow of water delivery between the lake and the small swamp lake across the gravel road behind the storage shed. The ground was soft and marshy and messy nearly all the time. Most of the kids liked the ambiance. However, it sure messed up the tennis shoes, if they were even worn. The experienced folks would wear rubber boots. The locals wore boots that almost came to their knees. Coy had worn old tennis shoes, and his feet seemed to always be a little damp. One of the first things Coy would do at the nightly campfires was to dry off his shoes, socks, and feet.

Coy thought the location of the resort was another example of man picking the way by consideration of his own end results while once again ignoring the power from above and straddling the whole scheme of the foundation of human choices based upon looks and feel. Coy realized more each day that life appeared to be filled with inconvenience and apparently humans were born to live with endurance. The distraction of low land was accepted as just another vexing problem to overcome. The whole setting of the resort and people-gathering location became nothing more than an imposition highlighted by damp feet. After a few days, Coy didn't even notice his wet feet anymore.

Something stopped Coy near the lake access ramp before he continued his trek to the fish house. He glanced back to see which way Growler went. With mild skepticism regarding spotting Growler, his eyes found him. Growler was gesturing to a couple fellows standing in front of Cabin 2. As expected, the message was received somehow, and the guys took a few steps in the direction of the dock in front of the cabin. Coy chuckled to himself. However, he was no longer just amused by Growler's nonverbal communication but started to watch carefully all the actions. He was beginning to understand all the communication Growler excelled at without saying a word. This was becoming an endearing quality to watch. Maybe just eye contact and a little look was all it took to communicate and get the message across. From the gestures, Coy deduced Growler was informing them why the cabin was where it was and why it was different from the other cabins.

Cabin 2 was rented out only when all the other cabins were full. It was built twenty feet from the shoreline with little elevation change from the cabin to the lake. Each cabin had its own personality. Cabin 2's personality began and ended with a history of flooding and water damage issues. Being so close to the lakeshore, it was built on stilts, so the cabin flooring was two feet above grade. There was still the potential of flooding lake water rising to the floor level when the lake water was high. And if that was not annoying enough, small wild animals like raccoons, rabbits, and mice would nest under the cabin and make all sorts of noise at night. The ambience of Cabin 2 drove most people crazy and really drove the real city folk types crazy.

Coy turned his head west a bit and something and someone caught his attention out on Dock 3. It was the young lady about his age who was wetting her feet by swinging them back and forth at the end of the dock. Suddenly, he felt a strange feeling. It was a new feeling he began experiencing this spring when he came into the presence of girls. This strangeness started happening in the last few months. Just last fall, he was playing football at Lee Park near their home and started a wrestling match with one of the neighbor girls after she tried to intercept a pass. She was strong, fast, smart and just the type of person to want on a team but it always seemed when they picked teams, she and Coy were on opposite sides. He really liked her. She was fun to be around, and she helped him a bunch in school. She had friends, and Coy was a bit more introverted by nature, so it helped having a neighbor friend who would step up and help be around people and get him invited to join the crowd. Having her in his life helped him sometimes understand the value of how nice it was to be part of something outside himself.

However, this spring, walking home one day, she grabbed his hand to walk together and their relationship changed forever. The fingers did not meet up nicely and were awkward. The clumsiness added to the newness. He felt pangs and weirdness from head to toe from somewhere he could not identify when he was around her now. Coy never wanted to be physical and wrestle with her again. She also was maturing and so was he as hair was growing and sprouting all over his body, with the most noticeable hair on top of his big toes.

He was not even forty feet from another young beauty sitting on the end of the Dock 3 and the same familiar feelings pounded away down to his core. Like a normal twelve-year-old and most men in general, his discernment started with outward appearances and even from a distance, he could tell she was not bad to look at. He was not blind and could not help but notice.

Coy was lost in thought and daydreaming like a stone cold lonely statue. He was looking her way when his space and time was unexpectedly interrupted by Jimmy and Gary. They were a couple of boys, ages seven and nine from Cabin 3, whom Coy had been introduced to and befriended a couple of days before. Coy felt as old as Growler around these two but playing hot box with them and throwing the football and Frisbee around was still pretty fun. It was so tough being a kid and a grownup at the same time.

"Hey, Coy, whatcha doin?' Jimmy startled Coy, breaking into his private zone, and speaking up with an excitable tone.

Coy dropped the pail of fish. Gary started laughing.

"He's staring at Cousin Tess. They came in late last night." Gary half laughed out the answer and response at the same time. "Or as Jimmy likes to call her, Mother Teresa. She is always such a know-it-all and tries to always be such a goodie two shoes!"

"She is pretty, and pretty darn smart to boot," Jimmy jumped in, and then stopped as if it was a stated question.

Gary was the older brother, and he was the talker. Jimmy usually only talked to get response and acceptance. Jimmy would speak up most often when it was a one-on-one situation.

The moment vanished or, for sure, had been extinguished. Coy picked up the pail of fish and asked the boys if they wanted to come along and help. So, off to the fish house the trio trotted like a teacher with a couple disciples. It was like a train of young men with purpose. The fish house was empty and not being used, so Coy walked in with his proteges behind him and in step.

"Now, men, step back from the table as I figure out how we are going to accomplish the task at hand." Coy spoke with a commanding tone.

He looked around as if he had never been in the house before. It was all show, as he was in there the night before with Growler for over an hour cleaning fish for the "newbies" from Cabin 2 and this morning already as well. Growler did most of the hard work. Coy did the final cleaning and final touch up of the cleaned fish. The well-cleaned slabs of fish meat, once ready, were presented and given to the folks for their evening meal.

There were other times in the fish house when Coy was with Grandpa and/or Growler when he didn't take the time to really take a good look around. Most of his focus was on his fish cleaning mentors and how they were doing their jobs.

Up until this year, he was only an audience member while the older folks did the cleaning. Other times his responsibilities were to clean things up and empty the fish guts pail. This time he had graduated to becoming the leader and was the full force and in the game. In fact, being the leader made him feel like Captain Kirk.

Coy liked making good estimates of the configuration of life around him. By memory, he could tell anyone the exact measurements of his bedroom at home. He could recite the colors of the walls, the pictures, the type of dresser, the bed, the lamp, the alarm radio, and even the exact distance his sister was sleeping right on the other side of the bedroom door one room away. He never really thought about why he did this stuff. However, he thought that if this was a natural skill, it was best to use it. Without hesitation, he looked carefully around the fish house as soon as they stepped in the building. His imaginary alien antennae were on high alert.

Coy looked around the fish house more intently now that he had an audience with him. He concluded quickly with an abridged assessment because he knew he had an energetic, restless, youthful audience.

It was natural for the occupants standing in the fish house to look at and scope out the resort and people. As Coy was gaining experience, he could figure out the time and smell of day and the energy of the folks around the resort. The cabins were decrepit, but the people were the lifeblood of the resort, and they made the atmosphere real and alive. The noise in the air of kids or older folks, the smell of food being prepared, percolating coffee, the feeling of the air temperature, the crackling of a fire, the buzz of the flies, and the flutter of the butterflies all were signs of the moments of the days and evenings.

"Let me help. What do you want me to do?" Gary spoke up. Jimmy began to nod as if the whole world should know what he was thinking, and, more importantly, he wanted to fit in, and it always seemed he wanted to be obedient and part of something.

The table was a little over three feet above the rough concrete floor. Gary and Jimmy being about the same height, about forty inches or so, could barely see up and over the top of the table. Coy, being almost five feet tall, also had a hard time being comfortable working off the table. However, he knew he could show no weakness. Of course, he didn't want to show any weakness and never admit struggle. He especially did not want to show any weaknesses around these Pojken. He was pleased to use the word Pojken in a context where he was the superior one. However, he immediately felt a pang of guilt for some reason.

"Well, let's see," Coy responded, realizing that would have been the same response Grandpa would have said to him while learning new adventures and trying his hands or hand at grown up things. "Why don't the two of you stand one on each side of me and watch for a while? Once I am done gutting and preparing a couple for skinning, I will show Gary how to use the skinner, then we will turn them over to Jimmy for the important job of the final cleaning of all the guts. Boys, grab a pail and turn it over and put it next to the counter to stand on them. Jimmy, you can have the fish pail and we will set it close to the water hose and sink, and you will be responsible for the final cleaning to get all those tough guts and slimy connections out, which is most important. And Gary, you stand to my left and I will hand you fish to skin. Will that be okay?"

"Sure thing, boss!" Gary responded for the duo as usual.

Jimmy was not quite as enthusiastic. Coy dumped the fish out on the table and turned over the pail and set it on the ground for Jimmy. Jimmy grabbed the side of the sink area and stepped up on the pail and leaned on the table, and he was now taller than Coy. He immediately did the expeditious look around and outside the fish house, and with an earsplitting shout, said, "Hey I can see the Frisbee in the tree, Gary! When we are done, let's see if Coy will help us get it down."

"Makes sense to me, Pojken," Gary responded.

Coy was taken aback as there was that Pojken word again. Coy felt guilty that he possibly may have taught Gary how and when to use the word. He pondered and wondered how in the world Gary would have known what that Pojken word stood for. He thought that even Gary seemed to know the word and, hopefully, when they were done here, he would not be a Pojken anymore.

"Okay, here we go. First, it is very important to have a sharp knife." Coy reached over to the front ledge by the screen window on the far side of the counter, which also worked as a small shelf. Knives, toothbrushes, and larger cleaning brushes for wiping down the table were stored there when they were not hanging on a nail on the wall. There were three different types of knives. Coy knew which one was best for cleaning sunfish, although all the knives were pretty beat up. Any avid serious fishermen would use their own when they cleaned fish. Coy then reached in front of Jimmy to his right onto the ledge next to the door, where the sharpening stone was kept. He sharpened the knife as best as he knew how by following the same pattern, he saw Growler use the night before. He remembered Grandpa saying that everything in the fish house started with the right tools and sharp knives.

Coy thought that it just seemed that all the good stuff in life came from experience and watching others for how things got done. *Well, at least if you consider cleaning fish in the "good stuff" category.*

Coy wanted to get done with this teaching experience expediently without incident. Although he was experienced, he had a twinge of nervousness for some reason. He was unsure where that feeling was coming from. His anxieties were on high alert. His nervousness grew very fast when a new voice entered the zone and startled him, just as he was cutting into the first fish.

CHAPTER 18

Then Came Tess

"Hey, what is your name?" The sweet sound came from a young beauty who had entered the fish house zone beyond the screen in front of Coy.

Startled, Coy looked up briefly and did not respond immediately, but continued working on the fish. He finished up his part of the process and asked Gary to hand him another to clean.

"We don't clean our fish that way," the young beauty continued.

"Really, this is how we do it here," Coy responded, without looking up this time. He stayed focused on his task at hand. Besides, he was a little nervous, and the best way to avoid an awkward confrontation was to give it little time and less effort. At least that worked sometimes. Furthermore, he had a sharp knife in his hand, and he knew that he had to concentrate.

"Do you want me to show you how it's to be done the right way?" she went on.

Coy stopped and looked up directly at her and immediately recognized her as the young beauty he spotted sitting out on the end of Dock 3 a few minutes before. They were three feet from each other, but separated by the screen. Coy appreciated the prodigious barrier of separation. He was in, and she was out. His thoughts were messed up and suddenly, he could not remember or have the ability to say anything. He realized his mouth had become very dry for some unknown reason.

In the brief glimpse at her, he gleaned immediately she was about the same age and size as himself. He thought that at least she seemed to be about the same size or so. He noticed from his glance that she had very nice hair, beautiful teeth, and absolutely beautiful ocean blue eyes that could stop time. Boy, did he notice.

He looked down more fervently and went about the business of cleaning fish. However, memories popped up in his mind of being at family and church picnics and outings, and it always seemed to Coy people generally migrated to people of the same age or, in some cases, the same physical size or appearance. Coy did not mind being with the kids, but he would eventually head back to the cooking and kitchen to listen in and be around the women folk. To Coy, women were much more thought-provoking and interesting, and they seemed to have the world figured out somehow better. The men usually sat around and talked about work or football or puffed-up chest stuff or women. Over time, without even knowing why, he became much more comfortable around the women or girls. However, this young lady was throwing a wrench into that theory. He was feeling anxious for some unknown reason. He did not like or understand the feeling. He did not like feeling something where he did not have any understanding and, more importantly, control.

Coy had a natural inclination to always think the best and make the best out of all situations. Therefore, he decided to be nice and supportive and be the social butterfly that Grandpa informed him would be one of his duties. He spoke eventually with the spontaneous shyness which was his usual way with newcomers in his life zone.

"Well, okay. That would be nice," Coy answered politely, as he looked up slightly with his eyes only, and spoke softly to the very noticeable beauty beyond the screen barrier.

"Those are some nice-sized fish there. My father used to fillet the bigger sunfish because they were so much easier to eat that way," she said with authority but with a soft, welcoming tone.

"Lovely," was all that Coy could think to respond through his slightly gritted teeth, not meaning to be condescending in any way.

Coy started cutting into the next fish and somewhere from within his soul, he now started feeling sorry for the fish. He wondered if the fish had feelings. Did the fish eyes see him coming at them with the knife? He had no idea why these thoughts popped into his mind. Oh well, he continued, and the noise of breaking the backbone as he cut into the next fish didn't bother him anymore. Besides, he was the man of the house, and he did not want to show weakness. He carefully muted his internal speaking thought of, "What the heck is happening to me right now?"

"Hey, hey, Jimmy is not doing his job." Gary interrupted Coy's uncomfortable thought process.

"Oh, okay, I'm sure Jimmy is doing fine. Let's take a look. Gary, you worry about your job; I will check on Jimmy and thank you," Coy responded, with his leadership position well in hand.

Coy grabbed one of the fish Jimmy had put in the clean water bowl to see how he had done it.

"Jimmy, this one is not quite finished up. See that white stuff, and that little yellow thing there hanging, we need to make sure that is all cleaned up," Coy instructed.

"Oh yeah. Sorry, sir. I forgot and will try harder," Jimmy politely and meekly responded.

Coy reached up and took an old toothbrush down from a nail on the vertical divider between the end of the screen window and the sidewall. He noticed the young beauty watching him closely when he looked up to find the toothbrush. He took the fish Jimmy had in his hand and thoroughly brushed the final pieces of guts off and completed washing the fish with the running water from the sink.

"Now, that is what it should look like, kid. Got it?" Coy patted Jimmy on the left shoulder as he looked at him.

"Will do, sergeant!" the little guy happily responded.

"Hey, Coy, show me how to use this skinner thing again, please. I can't figure it out," Gary said. Coy remembered thinking the day before that sometimes something that seemed so natural, like a quick jump over a little brook, was not an inconvenience but a habit but to others, it might be a chore.

Coy took his eyes off the fish in his hands and set it down on the counter. He looked out the side screens and beyond the young beauty to get a bigger view of what was going on before him. He glanced over toward the south side of Cabin 5. He took a glance west and looked over past Cabin 6, and then at Cabin 7. The break from the moment helped him jump back into the game with confidence. Confidence he needed right then and right now.

Coy turned to Gary, who now entered the game, and grabbed the fish from Gary's hands.

"Okay, find the edge of the top of the fish. Usually, there is a bit of loose skin, put the skinner right there, tighten your grip, and wind down on the handle." Coy talked while skinning one side of a fish for Gary.

"Wow, that is cool, man," Gary said.

Coy turned back and grabbed the fish he was working on to finish up his part of the cleaning, and he glanced up to see if the young beauty beyond the screen barrier was still there, and she was. "You said that your father used to clean, I mean fillet fish, didn't you?"

"Yes, I did," Tess retorted.

"I suppose you do all the cleaning now, huh?" Coy said while he looked down with a little snide smile.

"Ya, Ya," she said with hesitation, paused, and slowly said with a not-so-sweet voice, "No, he cannot clean fish anymore." She was obviously trying not to show emotion or reaction. Her voice had a perceptible gentle cracking sound.

"Oh, I am sorry. Is he hurt or something?" Coy recognized and spoke with a comforting tone.

"No, he is dead!" she sputtered anxiously. She stopped moving and began to think about a feeling she was grappling with: *dead*. She was realizing that when death took a father, it stole and changed the definition of the word *dead* forever—forever.

Coy looked up right into her now noticeably tearful, beautiful, deep ocean blue eyes. He recognized that if the Pacific Ocean had a story connected to each drop of blue water, he knew the story would be able to start and end with those eyes. He had no idea why he thought that but down deep, he felt it.

The conversation went silent. During this whole time, the boys finished cleaning the seven fish. Jimmy was finishing up the final cleaning process and getting more wet from the waist up with every fish he worked on. Gary finished cleaning up the skinner and hung it back up on the wall where Coy had taken it down earlier. Coy inspected the tables, guts bucket, the floor, and the hanging tools and began washing his hands with the hose.

"Aren't you going to say something, or anything?" she said as she stared right at Coy, just a foot or so away from the screen. Then she moved forward as close as she could get to the screen, with her nose pushing into the screen, waiting desperately for a response.

"I am sorry. I really do not know what to say or know you very well and that seems so personal. I am really sorry I brought it up, um, brought it up... hey, by the way, what is your name anyway?" "Tess," she softly responded.

"I do not know anybody named Tess. That is a pretty name, ma'am," Coy unconsciously responded. He wanted off the subject, but he knew it was important to be pleasant. He did not know why he was trying to be nice, but something or someone inside told him to be nice. His mother's advice again was always right there when needed.

"Say, what are you doing after lunch?" Coy jumped right back into his social director role.

"Nothing much, just hanging out and around the cabin," Tess responded. "Why, do you want to do something?"

"Like what?" Coy said.

"Well, do you play cards? We could play a game, or throw the Frisbee or something, or something else you might like to do."

"Whatever works for you is fine with me," Coy responded.

"Okay, maybe in an hour or so. Hey, have you ever played Scrabble?" she asked.

Coy reckoned that this could be his opportunity, something like catching the most or the biggest fish and just like Scrabble, it took a little time and patience and a little smart. Coy considered himself somewhat of a Scrabble expert, and he also knew that no one back home would even play with him anymore.

"Sure, that would be fun. Scrabble you called it? I can give it a try, thanks," Coy demurely responded. "What cabin are you at anyway?"

"We are in Cabin 4, but let's meet up in Cabin 5. That's where we play games," Tess demurely responded.

With that, Tess turned toward the cabins and walked away. Coy could not help watching her walk away until she was out of sight. He knew there was a strong possibility he had one on the line, and there was a good chance it was a very beautiful keeper. Coy couldn't have known it, but Tess was thinking the same thing.

Jimmy and Gary stepped out of the house. Coy gave the house the final spray down. He hooked up the hose, wrapped it around the spigot, and walked out of the house with the cleaned fish in a small saucepan. Gary was carrying the pail that was used to bring the fish to the house.

"Gary, would you bring the pail down to Dock 2, the one over there?" he instructed while pointing at the dock that could not be seen but was right in front of Cabin 2.

"Sure, Captain!" Gary replied with pride, and Jimmy followed him as they took off on their new journey.

"Hey, I'll figure out how to get that Frisbee down from the tree and will meet up with you boys later today, I mean, team," Coy shouted their way.

"Awesome!" they replied in unison.

Coy started his trek back to Little Mora.

CHAPTER 19

Back to Little Mora -Those People

———◉———

"Fate, like the Lord, moves in mysterious ways," and "Fate runs its own course," were the thoughts bouncing around in Coy's mind as he remembered his mother's words of wisdom again as he crossed the two-track road behind cabins. He was within earshot of Little Mora and already heard the sizzling of the fry pan and caught the smell of bacon frying coming from the cabin. He observed Grandpa filling the riding lawn mower with gas, parked on the south side of the cabin.

Growler, with astute anticipation, knew when the fish would be ready to fry, and he was prepared. Coy noticed more and more Growler seemed to be a step or two ahead in any game he was involved in. Coy raised his arm and waved to Grandpa with an acknowledgment that he was back at camp. Grandpa looked up, moved his head up and down without really looking at Coy, and stayed focused on what he was doing. Coy knew the message was accepted and received.

Coy grabbed hold of the screen door handle and began to speak as he stepped into Little Mora. "All ready to go, sir," he said as he entered the cabin while looking at Growler working the bacon on the stove.

Growler gave him the familiar sideways look with his head tilted down without saying anything, as they were back to communicating without words again. Growler gave a wily glance at the pan of fish Coy had in his left hand. He raised his left eyebrow like Spock would have, and Coy took that as, "Bring the fish over here as I am almost ready for the main course of action." Coy approached, and Growler touched the left arm of his young protege and handed him the spatula. Coy knew what that meant. He was to finish the task at hand, like an eagle pushing her young out of the nest to fly alone.

Growler stepped aside and walked over to the icebox to see if there was anything else to serve with the fish. He took out the knife attached to his belt and with one quick fluid movement, cut a chunk of butter off the side of the slab in the icebox. He handed Coy the butter with knife and all. "Here you go," he said with a quiet, calm tone. Coy carefully grabbed the knife from the older man, and their hands touched slightly.

This man really did not have any communication handicap to Coy. Growler did not have to talk to communicate. However, Coy really wanted to hear more from him. He was starting to sense people judged others so severely when there were perceived weaknesses. Especially weaknesses that could not be heard or strengths that could not be grasped. Coy did not want to be one of those folks on any side of the equation.

Coy was becoming more annoyed by the way people would judge others as a way to feel better about themselves. *People seemed to be in a constant state of comparison analysis or something like that*, he thought. He did not want any part of it. "This is who I am," came out of his mouth more and more around family and friends.

Coy had started taking the bacon out of the fry pan right at that sweet spot time, just before the burn when bacon was perfectly fried to a crisp. He deposited a small spatter of butter from Growler's knife in the pan and turned down the heat. He then reached up to the shelf right above the stove where the flour/cornmeal mix was stored, and dumped a small pile on a plate he grabbed from the shelf to the right of the stove. He rolled the newly cleaned fish into a bowl with beaten eggs, which Growler had prepared and handed him. He put each fish carefully in the mix, one by one. By the time he completed that task, the bacon/butter mix was the perfect temperature and condition. He then added the extra butter that he had received from Growler right in the bacon grease. It sizzled in the pan and he knew it was the right time. He always liked the initial little spark from the bacon grease. He looked to make sure the heat of the stove was about in the middle of the pan, and it was. He knew it was just about the perfect time and temperature to fry up some fish. He waited until all the butter had melted and when a slight bit of smoke rose from the fry pan. The pan and ingredients were ready. He turned the heat down one notch on the burner and one by one, he neatly put the fish in the pan. He carefully shifted the fish back and forth with a fork, so they would not stick to the pan. He flipped the fish at the exact moment he could see a little sizzle on the sides and seasoned each side of the fish with just the right amount of salt and pepper. Once on the new side, he continued moving the fish back and forth with the fork, and after about a minute, he began checking to see if the fish were cooked. He did this by sticking the fork into the fillets to see if the fork would stick in the fish. He knew if the fork stuck, the fish were not thoroughly cooked and ready. Another life lesson from Mom.

While this was going on, Growler set a few plates and cups on the table. Growler then sat down on the bench on the door wall that the table slid up to so he could keep his eyes on Coy the whole time. Coy knew he was being watched and kind of liked it.

Grandpa entered the cabin along with Pretzel. Once all three of them were in the cabin, along with the dog, it felt a little crowded. It was generally only at mealtime and right before going to bed at night that they were all in the cabin together or when it was raining sometimes or when playing cards.

"So how did the seven-and-a-half work for you guys?" Grandpa asked as if spitting it out to the room and not particularly to either one of them. Grandpa was in the habit of speaking into space and not at one person or right to people.

"Really well. You did another great job, Grandpa." Coy spoke while still looking down at the pan.

"Good, did everything work okay, or did anything stick or anything else happen?" Grandpa inquired for some more information.

"No, nothing!" Coy looked quickly and directly at Grandpa for a second and answered with a little higher tone.

"Okay, is everything all right between us all now, or do I have to have Pretzel settle something or get Brownie in here to help settle something?" Grandpa asked, and chuckled at the same time as he sensed a little tension in the room.

Growler gave a little under growl. Grandpa looked at him and chuckled. Both the older gentlemen sat at their places. Coy served them by setting the plate of bacon and fish down. Growler already put the orange nectar drink on the table with the plates, cups, utensils, and set out a couple pieces of bread and butter.

One Lifetime Is Not Enough!

Nothing too fancy, just a few fish, a piece of bacon or two, and some bread with butter and orange nectar. Preparations in place, now the purpose and reason for being in the cabin, which was to eat, took place. Coy sat down and as he did, he looked at Growler and noticed he sat there for a couple seconds before he dug into the food and drink. Unless Coy was mistaken, it looked like he took the time to give thanks.

"Have you run into those people who came in last night? They are staying in Cabin 7." Grandpa broke the unexciting silence and the sounds of three people eating and drinking.

"No, no I have not," Coy replied, while looking at Growler with some unknown reason of expectation.

"Well, we haven't had their type of folks very many times before. I heard they can be pretty good fishers. Well, I guess," Grandpa said.

"What do you mean by those folks or their types, Grandpa?" Coy spoke as if jumping right back in the game with his inquiring personality.

"You know, those people, you know, blacks, you know... those people, those folks," Grandpa said.

"Really, Grandpa! What do you think they call you?" Coy responded.

"I really don't know. Probably that old white one-armed fart," Grandpa responded, and chuckled, then took a deep breath.

"So, what would you rather be known as, a fart or white?" Coy asked.

"Oh, you know what I mean, okay black folks," Grandpa responded with a smidgen of annoyance.

"No, not really, what would you prefer to be called?" Coy continued.

"I don't know," Grandpa replied with a little force and gave Coy a stern look.

"How about old, worn-out, pretty smart, white guy? But you really cannot be called a white guy, your skin is more of a wrinkled reddish brown or something. How about old almost black guy?" Coy said, knowing it might make Grandpa feel bad or something. The back and forth went on for a couple of minutes. With no winner, they just stopped. After they were done, Grandpa told them he was going to lie down for some shuteye and relax.

Coy and Growler did the dishes and cleaned up the lunch mess. They stepped quietly out of the cabin together. They looked at each other and went their separate ways. Coy decided to go to Cabin 5, and Growler toward the gravel road. Growler was carrying his small bag again. Coy would typically want to know what was in the small bag, but this time he let it go. *There was really no use following Growler now*, Coy pondered. After all, they would be out in the boat in the morning, and Coy wanted to take some time to think of the million questions that he wanted to ask and get answered.

One Lifetime Is Not Enough!

CHAPTER 20

The Invite—People Are People

It was time for Coy to answer an intriguing invitation. With that purpose, he trotted off to Cabin 5 like a horse that had just made a big jump in an arena filled with screaming fans. He found satisfaction that he fought back and stood up to Grandpa. However, he did not like the feeling he might have seemed disrespectful. He continued to assume Grandpa liked his spunk. The distraction of the previous discussion and conversation with Grandpa was just the right panacea. After all, he could not help but be nervous about meeting up with Tess over at Cabin 5.

Coy was always bothered when people labeled others based upon some external distinguishable description, such as skin color. The whole idea engaged an ache deep in his soul. He thought about what other folks might label him. Mom told him not to let any of that bother him, but it did. Something as ridiculous as never trying on a baseball cap in front of friends because he knew he had a big head. He rarely went without his shirt because he was conscious of his little belly. He wondered if his eyes were really brown because they were full of it. Coy never wanted to put anyone in an uncomfortable situation. He tried not to put himself in an uncomfortable situation ever, even when friends or family gathered and wanted to call people names based upon nationality, race, religious upbringing, or economic status. Coy would walk away from being part of those conversations. His adult thoughts and passions were growing stronger each and every time, and he fought back on this day.

He slowly ambled his way to Cabin 5. He made a list of imperfections he could think of. Bad-hair guy, spotted-skin woman, birthmark punk, overweight girl, pink lady, red woman, yellow man, black people, white people, all popped up in his mind. He knew the list would be exhaustive if he really went at it. But all that popping up in his mind was simply the human tendency to judge others by their looks or skin color, height, weight, body type, or anything. What was stewing in Coy's mind was that humans had no choice or nothing to do with anything that distinguished them from others, such as skin color or, for that matter, being a woman or a man. They just were who God made them and wanted them to be.

"People are people." Coy spoke out loud with confidence.

He remembered his teacher from Sunday school saying Jesus Himself went to Egypt, and from all the pictures at school all those folks who lived in Egypt appeared to be black-complexioned. Coy was sure he hadn't heard about Jesus prejudging anybody. There wasn't any physical description of Jesus in the Bible so as far as Coy was concerned, Jesus might have been a dark-complexioned man.

Coy was realizing it took patience and skill to disentangle the things people learned from life, from others, and from themselves. Coy lived with the hope he would learn the right way somehow, some way. However, when one was twelve and had been around a while, one just did not have to believe things on the local authority, even though the authority was trustworthy. Coy thought it was time for him to have an opinion.

Coy naturally and without hesitation found himself taking a shortcut to Cabin 5 by jumping over Chelsea Brook without even having to think about it, instead of going the long way around and walking over the simple six-foot-long bridge built with two-by-sixes by Cabin 1. His mind was swirling with thoughts. Something was going on. He wanted to go see the folks in Cabin 7. His immediate thoughts were that they surely must be okay as they were living and enjoying life right there, right now, and right where they all were. But that meet and greet would have to wait. It was now time for him to teach a lesson to the young lady waiting for him in Cabin 5. He was ready to deliver a lesson in the game of Scrabble.

He moseyed on close behind Cabin 5, and he could hear the splashing and noises of some younger kids swimming between Docks 4 and 5. It was Gary and Jimmy and their two younger sisters, Sandy and Cindy.

Cabins 3, 4, and 5 had large front windows facing the lake and were close in proximity to each other, as if related, likely built around the same time. When someone walked on the worn path in front of the cabins, the people inside the cabins could see who was outside and who was moving around. Tess was sitting on the sofa facing the window and saw Coy as he walked in front of Cabin, over to the door on the west side of the cabin. She met him at the door. He stepped in the cabin and realized it was somewhat awkward for him, as he usually did not intrude on the folks in the cabins. He had, of course, been in the cabins many other times with Grandpa, freshening them up, along with resupplying the bed linens.

"Hi, young man, how are you doing? Thank you for coming over." Tess politely greeted Coy while turning and starting to walk the other direction.

"I am doing great and thank you for the invite." Coy kept the politeness going.

Cabin 5 had two bedrooms, and the first bedroom was behind the wall at the entrance. The large sofa was up against that wall and sitting directly opposite the front window that faced the lake. Ten feet into the cabin was the kitchen, where there was a table with six chairs.

Tess was already in the kitchen and Coy followed right behind her. He rounded the corner behind his hostess and found a new, big snag in his well- thought-out battle plan right in front of him. There were three other girls from somewhere between eight to fourteen years of age in the kitchen.

Interesting, he thought. This might be a bit more amusing and perhaps more difficult of a task than he first expected. He generally did not ever feel hemmed in when there were many people around as he could disappear in the noise of crowd. He was the only boy with these girls, and getting lost in the crowd was probably not going to be an option. He thought even a bumbling idiot would recognize getting lost when he was the only boy would be a tremendous challenge. He decided to just give up on that front.

The Scrabble game board was already set up on the table. Coy glanced at the table and the chairs around the table. He didn't need intuition to know the cards might be stacked, so to speak, against him. He did appreciate the competition exhibition and arena was in place and ready.

Two of the girls were already sitting down in chairs. Tess sat down in one of the empty chairs nearest the counter area and looked at Coy and invited him to sit down in the chair next to her. To Coy, it was like a queen guiding the king to sit down on the throne next to her.

The game was afoot with instructions given. One of the young ladies was fiddling with the tiles and starting to be distribute them as Tess introduced Coy to all the girls and the girls to Coy. In the brief introduction, Coy learned the three other girls were all sisters and on vacation with their family for the week, and many extended family members and friends were there. They were all in Cabins 3, 4, and 5.

Coy was in his shy disposition mode. He knew even if it looked like he was trying to be timid, it was pretend as it was more than a show this time. In his anxious life moments, he realized he had one of his mother's great qualities: the ability to be busy. He decided to take a good look at the competition in front of him and assess his challengers with the intention of deciphering the situation, doing something to help him overcome his anxiety over it. He used the Growler technique of holding his head down for an appearance of humility while looking up with his eyes occasionally. He liked this technique, so he used it. Acting humble when not humble was a newfound learning experience for Coy. He was not too sure about it but for some reason, Coy felt this might be the time to try it out.

Tess introduced the girls to Coy and she started with Ruby as the oldest sister. She was fourteen years old, very pretty and to Coy, she looked like she was right out of a Disney movie as the leading beautiful blond-haired maiden. Coy could not help but notice she was a stunning beauty. Ruby blushed a bit, which must have been a natural response to noticing Coy's look. Her cheeks were getting a little red. Coy smiled and noticed the blond hair, beautiful to a point of distraction, and a delightful smile. Tess moved on and introduced the young lady sitting next to Ruby.

Her name was Molly. Coy could see she was a little bigger and taller than Ruby. Tess informed him that she was Ruby's younger sister and twelve years old. She was also blond with a bit lighter color. Coy could tell right away she had some spunk. She had a cute dimpled smile with an instantly warm feel producing a delightful presence.

Tess looked past the table and over toward the youngest sister, Pearl, who was sitting on the bench away from the table and under the south window of the cabin. She had curly, darker blond hair. He immediately noticed her warm smile and endearing eyes. He estimated she was about seven or eight years old. He always looked at the hair, smile, teeth and especially the eyes, and everything about Pearl looked perfect.

Coy was beginning to get a funny feeling inside. The ambience of the environment was a shade above Coy's pay grade. He usually was comfortable around girls, and these people were just girls, he thought, after all.

Coy knew they were all quite cute and had a much better cleaned-up look than he had, especially after the undertaking of his busy morning. He was practicing not judging by outward appearances, but he thought at least he could notice they were cute and nice. Judging from the way they were giggling and fidgeting with their hair, they did not mind Coy being around and noticing them too. Tess was still the most distracting to Coy. He could not get over her eyes. They were so deep, blue, and beautiful and, along with her brunette hair, there was just something very special about her to Coy.

He tried his best to show that he did not notice that the girls might have been flirting at him. He sat up straight in his chair and looked ready for battle. He did a quick what he hoped was an unnoticed sniff movement to his underarms and hands when none of them were looking to make sure he was at least presentable and blew his breath into his palms to make sure his breath did not smell. He was not really very satisfied with any of his discoveries.

The introductions and the warmup were over. Coy, without any savvy, could not help but think that he had it in him to handle this situation and these girls. He thought all he had to do was to keep levelheaded and not get ahead of himself as his mother would have told him. His confidence was still high, which helped him get over some of his anxiety. However, it did not take very long to change as his mind was a scrambled with angst. There were just too many distractions. He realized quickly he could not even figure out how to spell his own name or figure out the point totals of even a short three-letter word, such as coy.

Coy's process toward a higher education always started with confidence in all situations. "When it counts, performance under pressure is what makes the difference," was what the football coach from his team he was on last fall told them before their last game. "This is game time, so leave the distractions at home or school, men!" He spoke softly to himself what the football coach told the team right before kickoff. For a brief moment there was no talking around the table, and it was silent.

Tess broke the awkward silence and said, "We had better pick teams."

Pearl immediately spouted. "He smells!" The girls all started laughing with a muted undertone.

Coy did have to admit it, little Pearl was spot on. It all at once dawned on him again that it had become a very busy and hectic day. He did chores early in the morning, walked around the resort, and then was sidetracked with the test ride in the boat with Growler. Most importantly, he experienced a massive awakening of a new level with Growler's communicating by talking. After all that, he ended up cleaning fish and helped prepare lunch.

Coy was about to start a game of Scrabble in Cabin 5 with four girls and he didn't have time to jump in the water off Dock 1 and take a quick resort bath. He enjoyed the resort baths and, at least once a day, he jumped into the lake to refresh and clean the smell off. In summary, he knew he could not help but smell, especially with all the spraying of water and teaching in the fish house with the boys. There was no doubt some overspray that went on with the boys got on him. Usually, none of this would be a bother. For some odd reason, his memory flashed back to the atomic bomb training back when he was in first grade, where the siren went off and everyone was told to get under their desks. Coy remembered how stupid that was, as being in proximity of a bomb going off meant everyone would probably be dead anyway. By the time Coy came to from his reverie, Ruby and Molly were spraying some sort of air freshener on him. He just let them and did not say anything.

Coy began to speak what he was ready to say with his typical attempt at spontaneous shyness, which was his usual way with people in new situations. "Thanks," was all he could muster. He hoped his outward actions said the same.

"That may have helped a little, but now we have a bad smell that we can tell is covered up with a good smell, and the bad smell is winning just a snippet. Oh well, good for now," Tess said. Coy frowned a little, with the thought that Tess did know he smelled.

"Good grief, Tess! A snippet? So, where are you from?" Molly, the most outspoken of the group said, while looking at Coy.

Coy thought he remembered it was his time to answer something.

"From the cities; I am going into seventh grade." Coy's response startled Ruby and Molly.

"Are you here with your parents? Or, I mean do you live with those two old guys? Or are you related to the resort owner or something?" Molly pressed on.

Pearl interrupted, "Hey, does anyone else want some salt water taffy?" "I am okay," Coy responded.

Coy reached into his pocket for one of the pink soft mints Grandpa always had out to share in a bowl on the table in Little Mora, and put it in his mouth. Coy loved those mints and every time he ate one, it refreshed his mouth and breath and reminded him of Grandpa and Grandma.

The girls grabbed a couple pieces of taffy from the bowl that Pearl, who desperately wanted to be one of the girls, was sharing.

"The old man with the one arm is my Grandpa, and the other fellow is a friend or someone from the family. And no, we are not related to the resort owner, at least I don't think so." Coy suddenly felt like a child struggling futilely to break the code of an adult conversation with only limited facilities and knowledge. Like school and confirmation classes, it always seemed like the girls asked the most and best questions. Coy always felt he had something to ask but would not remember what until later. Most of the time he would remember and then silently recite his questions to himself on the way home. He ended up stopping his response with that.

Pearl had decided, with a little guidance and encouragement from her sisters, to be a spectator. She was not ready for Scrabble as they played with her already this morning to make sure she knew she was part of it all. They knew and, more importantly, Pearl realized she might not be quite ready to play. Pearl wanted to be part of something, and it was better she made her own decision to participate by watching. The other girls encouraged and supported her decision.

Pearl looked over at Tess and said, "Hey, when did your daddy die? And how?"

The question instantly shook Tess and rattled her back a bit. Ruby tried politely with her eyes and hand actions to scold Pearl for asking such a question.

"Hey, what did Mom say? In time we can ask, right Pearlie...?" Molly added.

"Oh, I am sorry, Tess," Ruby responded as she thoughtfully glanced at Tess. Pearl meekly responded with a warm smile to Tess. Tess turned her head and stared out the window.

"That's okay. We do not know exactly when he died, but we do know he died a few months ago over somewhere that away... you know east. I think by China or somewhere." Tess gestured with her head. She kept staring out the window as if she was looking for something or someone.

"Was he fighting in the war?" Ruby, now engaged in the conversation, asked.

"Yeah... he was." Tess's voice cracked as she responded. She did not even have to say the word, Vietnam.

"That is enough for now, and let's play teams. Who wants the boy?" Ruby responded, knowing it was time to ease the tension of the conversation.

Tess immediately spoke with her back to them, while still staring out the window and with an undertone of a giggle, "I'll take the boy. We all know he will obviously need some help."

Tess turned from staring out the window and made eye contact with Coy at the exact time he looked at her. Their unspoken thoughts toward each other were in a glance and laugh. The whole group giggled and laughed. While Coy laughed, he looked at Tess with a modest shy smile. She received the message.

"That seems to work for him. We will maybe be okay," Tess responded.

Ruby and Molly began to allocate and fiddle with the tiles. Coy took the time to take a quick smell of his sleeve and under his armpits again. He confirmed that he did smell. The air freshener was just barely working.

Coy thought the best way for him to act right now was to not let on too much he was pretty good at Scrabble. He decided to defer the team questions and thought processes to Tess. Down deep, he knew he wanted Tess to take the lead, especially if it made her feel better.

Tess and Coy were first to play. She was deep in thought as she scanned over and organized their letter tiles. He looked over at the tiles and tried to come up with something. He found he was too distracted in this setting. He was left with complete blankness of thought.

"Hey, where is China?" Pearl asked as if speaking to the room. She looked out the small kitchen window above the sink, where just a few minutes before Tess looked out.

Ruby looked over to Pearl to make sure that she was paying attention, and pointed out the window that was almost straight due east direction. "That a way," Ruby said.

"What? To that cabin?" Pearl responded.

"No goofball. A long way that way, Pearlie girl, like thousands of miles that way." Molly answered this time.

"Why was your daddy in China anyway?" Pearl pushed a little more as she asked the question, looking over at Tess.

"He was fighting the war, you know, the Vietnam War." Tess answered without looking up from their tiles.

"What's a Vietnam?" Pearl continued her inquisitive questions.

"It's not a what; it's a place, Pearlie." Molly jumped back into the conversation.

"Why is there a place called Vietnam where daddies go and die?" Pearl innocently continued.

Tess pushed her chair back from the table. The whole room felt the sadness. Coy looked directly into her eyes and knew those beautiful blues eyes were much too beautiful and serious for her age. He sensed there might be a tear present and, naturally, he knew what likely was about to happen. "Hey, I do smell! Do you lovely ladies mind?" Coy bellowed out while laughing.

It broke the heavy moment. They all giggled, even Tess. There was cheer in the room again.

"Hey, do you guys keep that radio in the window going all the time?" Coy asked.

"Yes," Ruby answered.

"What type of music do you listen to?" Coy asked.

"Well, there seems to be only two stations that come in up here, KKIN out of Aitken and WDGY out of Brainerd. We keep it on WDGY because it plays rock and roll, and Mom and Dad like that music better," Ruby said.

"That's great station. The only station Grandpa ever wants to listen to is KKIN with the country and western music and Paul Harvey. I do like it and I kind of enjoy Paul Harvey, because then Grandpa and I talk about what Paul had to say. Good day!" Coy ended.

"Good what?" Molly said.

"Good day, that is the way Paul Harvey always ends his broadcast. You know, good day, right?" Coy responded.

"Oh, okay. Well anyway, let's play." Ruby jumped back into the conversation.

Tess was now leaning forward and engaged in thought while looking at the letter tiles. "Okay, let's see just how smart you really are, Coy," she whispered into Coy's ear.

Coy realized this group might be way above his pay grade. He had just learned what that pay grade statement meant the night before by the fire. He still did not know precisely what it meant, but it seemed to fit in this circumstance. That was all he could think about right then. He did remember Grandpa saying to him sometimes it was just how the cards fell. He was not quite sure what that meant either, but it seemed right for this moment.

He leaned over near Tess and whispered softly, "We have the word *create* in our tiles, did you see that?"

Tess leaned into him while looking at the tiles and said, "Yes, yes we do, that will work, thanks." She was also distracted by the moment and conversation.

"You okay, Tess?" Ruby asked.

"Yeah, Yeaaah, I was thinking about what Mom said to me this morning," Tess went on.

"What was that?" Ruby asked.

Tess looked around the room and at all the girls and Coy and said, "Well, Mom and I were talking about Daddy, and she told me last time they were together they were fighting over money or something, or a combination of something or something, whatever. She told me the last thing she ever said to him as he was leaving home to fight in that stupid war was, 'Have you had enough?' And she told me he said yes, and she said, 'You know what, I have also had enough for a lifetime.' She then told me right when he was getting in the car that was there to pick him up, she shouted at him, 'One life is just not enough!' She told me this morning she will regret her choice of words for the rest of her life." Tess stopped and looked down for a moment to reflect and said, "One life is just not enough!"

The whole room was mesmerized and taken aback. Tess was crying. The entire group felt the drops of tears. Tess would be the only one able to break it up, and she did so as she wiped her tears from her face on her sleeve and said, "Let's not talk about that anymore and have some fun and concentrate on the game." She looked at each of them at the table with a big smile.

Coy, who also had tears in his eyes, looked the other way and wiped the tears off. After he did, he realized his whole face smelled. Coy realized Grandma was right again: *Everyone you meet might be fighting a hard battle—and maybe harder than your own.*

As Coy was thinking this thought, the radio announcer from the small transistor radio sitting on the windowsill said, "The next song we'll play was the number one hit at this time four years ago in July of 1969—The Archies' 'Sugar, Sugar.'"

Tess and Ruby also caught the announcement and immediately they jumped up and said together. "Let's be the Archies and sing along. Turn the radio up."

Coy loved this song, especially after they put it on the back of the Super Sugar Crisp box. Coy and his sister wore the little plastic record down, playing it so many times while singing along. Coy would pretend to be Archie or Reggie when needed, but mostly Archie. Sometimes when he was alone, he would play the drums and pretend to be Jughead. His sister would play Betty and, of course, Veronica. She resembled and had the Veronica look. When the neighborhood kids got together, one of the pretty girls would be Sabrina at the kissing booth. And for a moment, Coy reminisced and missed his friends and sister.

But these girls would do, and this could be fun. He immediately jumped up and said, "I will be Archie."

Tess said, "I will be Veronica."

Molly spoke up and said, "Well, I can be Betty."

Pearl just looked on and did not quite get it. She was only four when the song was a hit but that did not mean she didn't want a piece of the action, and she said, "Let me be someone."

Ruby looked at Pearl and said, "Of course, you can be either Jughead or Reggie, Pearlie. They are boys, but that is okay. Which one would you like to be?"

Pearl gave her older sister a warm yet funny look and said, "How come I have to be a boy?"

"It's just pretend and for fun, Pearlie, so go with it," Ruby responded.

Coy then said. "I can be both Archie and Reggie, how about you be Jughead and pretend to be the drummer? That is a really important part, Pearlie." Both Tess and Ruby looked at Coy and appreciated his kindness and response.

The commercials on the radio for Tide laundry detergent and other products and services were over. The beginning of the song started. They played the actual Archies song, where Archie asked Sabrina to watch from the kissing booth at the beginning before the announcer at the bandstand announced the band, and Archie said, "Here is our new song," and the tune began. Coy was right on time.

Coy, Ruby, and Tess had already grabbed some spoons for microphones.

Coy started. "Sugar, ah honey, honey…" He was close to being on tune and on time and was careful not to be too loud as to over-sing the song playing on the radio.

The girls were laughing while enjoying and singing along.

Then Molly hit the Betty part perfect with the sweetness, exactly like Betty did in the cartoons.

Coy went on, then Tess hit the Veronica part perfectly with a high squeal tone.

Coy was playing with his fake guitar, and so was Tess when she jumped in and played Reggie. She even had the crabby Reggie look on her face.

Pearl drummed along with the beat with her imaginary drum set.

The song was just under three minutes, and they had a blast with smiles and joy. It was a moment of pure fun and enjoyment. Coy loved the feel and the fun of just being a kid. Tess smiled; she really needed to have a reason to smile. Ruby led the effort to perfection. Molly played up the pretty Betty wonderfully, and Pearlie not only enjoyed being in the band but sensed she had purpose.

The song was over and when they all looked at each other, there was a different feel and bond in the room. They had connection. They were all smiling and laughing. Coy, especially, appreciated the wide smile across Tess's face. She had a generous laugh combined with a warm smile encircling her eyes with tiny wrinkles, making her, paradoxically, look much younger yet older at the same time and even more beautiful to Coy. The room of friends knew that when Tess looked happy, it was time for everyone to take a back seat.

Coy etched the smile and look on Tess's face into his memory forever.

They dug deep and played Scrabble. The game went on for about an hour-and-a-half, and all of them did very well. Coy held his own. Although, he came to play and win and show off a bit, by the time the game started and after the introductions, tears, and jamming to "Sugar, Sugar," he wanted to just be friends. The girls gained some respect toward Coy and he to them.

He sensed it was time to move along. He needed to check in on Growler, and he needed to rest a bit before the early evening festivities. He politely excused himself and thanked each of them by looking right in their eyes.

"Thank you, fine ladies. It was truly my pleasure. Good day!"

Tess walked with him to the door and touched his left forearm and said, "Thank you, oh and by the way, I am called Tess. My mother has always called me Tess. However, my real and official name is Teresa. That is what my father always called me." Coy had never felt so thanked in all his life.

He stepped out of the cabin and decided to head to Dock 1. He needed to take a swim. Even he could not take his smell any longer. As he was walking to Dock 1 on the far east side of the resort shoreline, he felt a little like the girl running away in the Cinderella or Snow White story. Coy would always get those two stories mixed up.

CHAPTER 21

Emmanuel

The sun had been shining down on the earth for a few hours. Coy knew the water was that perfect afternoon warm temperature when it was drenched with a 95-degree sunny day. It was the perfect time for him to take his resort bath near and off the west side of Dock 1. He jumped in with all his clothes on because his clothes needed some washing too.

While splashing around and cleaning his face with lake water, he started thinking about what Growler might be doing. However, his peaceful ponder and wonder time was infiltrated.

"Hey, hi. What's your name?" flew in the air at him like the dragonflies he was ducking when his head was above water.

He looked up, and standing on the dock was a boy of about his age. His immediate thought was that this boy was obviously from Cabin 7.

"Coy," he replied.

"That's quite a name. I never heard that one before. Mine is Emmanuel, but my friends call me El."

"Hi, El, what's up?" Coy said, and spat out some water.

"We got in late yesterday. I'm walking around checking out the place," El said, and then paused and did a quick look around and continued. "Why did you jump in with all your clothes on?

"Because my clothes might have been smellier than me, I think," Coy quickly responded.

El laughed and so did Coy.

"Hey, what you are doing later? Do you want to hang out or something?" El asked.

"Not sure, I kind of want to take it easy for a while, then probably some chores or something," Coy responded.

"We are going to have a big campfire one of these nights by our cabin, which I think is Cabin 7. Stop by if you can, since I believe we are now friends. We can have some fun together," El invited.

"Thanks, I will stop by," Coy responded, remembering Grandpa had told him to be sociable with everyone.

Coy continued his bath. El turned around and walked off the dock and when he reached the shore, he turned and looked out at Coy and said, "Goodbye for now, my friend." He continued on his way, checking out the resort and surroundings.

Coy pulled off his shirt and cleaned under his armpits and finished up his bath by washing through his hair. He stepped over to the dock and pulled himself up out of the water and onto the dock. He decided to relax and lie on the dock to dry out as the afternoon sun was beaming down.

CHAPTER 22

Coy Becomes a Snoop

The afternoon sun was intense and hot but the light eastern breeze was refreshing and made the dock a pleasant place. Coy looked up and could see a glimpse of Grandpa walking toward the north side of Little Mora. From Dock 1, he could only see the north side of the cabin, as a large oak tree and Cabin 2 blocked the view of the front of the cabin and the fire pit area. Grandpa sauntered to the north side of the cabin and spotted Coy on Dock 1 and started walking and making his way toward him. Coy was relaxing and lying down on the dock half asleep. He heard someone coming and looked up briefly and saw Grandpa.

"Hey, Coy. Do you want to head down to Hilding's with Growler and me? We're going over there to pick up some eggs and bacon and give him a hello," Grandpa said, walking close to the shoreline and the end of the dock. Their eyes made contact, and Grandpa spoke up loudly again.

Coy awakened groggy from a brief nap and said, "What? I mean, ah, what did you say?"

"Hilding, you know Hilding? Do you want to go along with Growler and me and see him?" Grandpa asked again.

Coy realized his outer clothes were pretty dry, but his underwear was still wet and a little uncomfortable; it needed some more drying time, so he responded, "Nah, thank you, I think I want to hang out around here. Is that okay with you?"

"Of course, take it easy. Looks like you got yourself a good bath there. Good for you," Grandpa responded.

Grandpa taught him a week earlier about the resort bath. He appreciated it as much as Coy when Coy cleaned up. Coy, now past being startled by Grandpa entering his space, wiped off the sleep in his eyes, sat up, and continued, "No, go ahead, guys. I need a little more time." Grandpa had discernment and somehow understood. He turned around to start walking back to Little Mora and waved his stub arm and said, "Take it easy."

Coy waved back and started chuckling. He remembered back a few days before when he, Grandpa, and Growler went down over to Hilding's together. As they were leaving, Grandpa turned away with almost the same exact manner and said to Hilding, "Take it easy."

Hilding had an endearing and energetic personality that went along with his rough and slightly limited language and responded, "Take it easy! Are you kidding? That is what I did the last time, and I lost my job!"

Both Grandpa and Coy had laughed. Coy had looked at Growler and for the first time he perceived Growler had the ability to smile.

Grandpa loved telling that story and had told it to everyone he had been in contact with the past couple of days. It brought about enduring laughter.

Coy lay back down on the dock for a few more minutes. He picked himself up and felt refreshed and decided it was time to move on. He walked off the dock and jumped onto shore. His mind immediately recognized the opportunity. His clothes were about ninety percent dry and his underwear about fifty percent. However, he felt pretty good about it all. He knew this would give him a chance to explore through Little Mora and give him a possibility and chance to examine and maybe find something more about Growler. And just maybe, he thought, he could be brave enough to look over and around Growler's stuff, especially the book he saw by the lampstand.

Coy waited a few minutes and ambled his way slowly in the direction of Little Mora. Grandpa's El Camino was gone, and there was no one around. He moved to his destination with a stealthy purpose and carefully opened the door to Little Mora.

Coy lived with purpose and focus with an overwhelming mission to complete whatever pushed him past his comfort zones. He had discreetly entered the Little Mora Cabin and now stood in silence at the center of the small kitchen area, instinctively knowing from past experience the way to his destination even in the shadow of darkness. However, even with familiarity in hand, he was still filled with consternation and contemplation. His acute self-awareness confirmed he did not have a clue what he was doing or why he was doing it. His inquiring mind and youthful exuberance could not and would not be stopped.

Coy felt irreverent, like one of those altar boys who had just smoked a joint in the john. Nevertheless, he continued moving through the kitchen into the bedroom area, making his way directly to where the old man's memoir book was not-so-carefully hidden. His innate presumption told him it must have been left there and hidden just well enough to be found. He pulled the chain on the lamp and turned on the meager light while reaching down and picking up the book with care, knowing it deserved to be treated like a treasured possession which surely stood the test of time.

Coy carefully unwrapped the tie band from the book, which kept the well-worn pages and loose notes from spilling out, and sat down on the edge of the bed near the nightstand. He opened book and set it down on his lap and decided to let God choose where and what was to be read this day. After a brief moment, he started to peruse briskly through the pages and notes of the treasured mystery book, hunting for clues and, perhaps, unforeseen pearls. He let his fingers, eyes, and mind go to the pre-ordained pages God wanted him to read. He browsed through familiar first few pages and arrived to about the one-third portion of the book. His leading forefinger stopped, and he paused to whisper a needed prayer. He was feeling a twinge of guilt; twas as if Jesus had taken a swing at him. The prayer calmed his mind. He continued to reflectively examine the words written by an older man and pondered and passionately desired to know the where, when, and how moments in life when the well-traveled timeless words would have been written.

Coy stopped reading every so often to look up and around while straining to hear something hidden in the silence. He listened carefully and looked around for any noise or anyone or anything, as if someone or something else wanted to be in his space.

"Holy cow!" he whispered loudly, as his reflections exploded with too many thoughts. The words and language recorded in the book were difficult to read, understand, and comprehend, and he struggled mightily. He sat silently in thought, hoping the feeling of vulnerability was external, intentionally hiding his internal deliberations.

The story and mystery became vaster and more confusing each time Coy read from the mystery book. His sympathy grew deeper for this older man each time he read from his book. He was entangled with a devotion, bordering on obsession, for answers that fueled his unquenched thirst to understand this older gentleman who was dropped like an A-bomb into his life. His young mind cognitively recognized each glimpse with a desire to quench the thirsting of his heart to learn the truth and purpose.

Coy stopped again and looked around the room. He looked at the nightstand and, ironically, thought how the book was hidden neatly and in view on the lowest shelf. The bedroom was small with three twin beds and one window that gave barely enough daylight in the room to let him navigate through the book. There was one small lamp on the lone nightstand. The extra effort it took to read the welcomed expressions in the dim lighting invariably enhanced his concentration to read even more carefully and clearly for answers and meaning.

Coy was always pleased to discover the writing to be remarkably legible, albeit faint, but never dull. The wording was difficult for a twelve-year-old and obviously came from a very intelligent and perhaps educated man. Coy prayed silently again for direction and answers, and God directed him to a heading that grasped ahold of his attention. He began to read out loud quietly. The heading was dated April 12, 1961. He had a sensation of a light being switched on inside his head like a revelation with a strong feeling and belief that this was the perfect place to read. The date was his birth date and his aspiring ambition was rewarded with enlightenment.

And he read…

While he read his mind filled with emotions and revelatory explosions. He read for 20 minutes or so and tired and completed his reading with...

> *I am not afraid of dying. I am afraid of being dead. Show me a glimpse. The revelation of the moment becomes final with the realization that the only way to win the fight to retain victory is an embodiment of the thought, where the only way to survive and thrive is that one life is not enough. I pray You will not let death melt my pages away. My burning midnight oil is running low and that is it for now.*

Coy felt chockfull and his head would not let him read anymore. His brain was exploding in a fire of thoughts and was completely out of energy. Without knowing how or when it happened, he found himself kneeling next to the bed by the nightstand. He realized the position helped with the minimal light from the lamp. With book in hand, he realized he was in a praying position. He found, as of late, he was praying more and more, when in the past he only prayed when asked to or at church and rarely did he pray alone. Coy prayed silently and carefully put the wrap band back on the well-worn book, and he put the treasured book right back as close as possible to its original position on the lowest shelf of the nightstand. He stood up, rose from his position, and carefully and surreptitiously walked on his tiptoes out of the Little Mora cabin.

Coy did not even remember walking out of the cabin. He looked back at the door while standing right outside of Little Mora, and he was overwhelmed with thoughts and a yearning feeling. He looked around to see if anyone saw him stepping out of the cabin for no other reason than to see if he had entered a new world. He looked back at the door as if it was some unknown portal to a different world. He could not even remember opening the door, walking through the door, or closing it. Nonetheless, he had a revelation and understanding that a mystery rarely starts with the answers, or does it?

CHAPTER 23

Jordan's Bay Part One: The Entrance to Rebirth

It was Sunday morning a few days later in early July 1973. Coy was ready to accept the well-anticipated invitation to go fishing with Growler out in Jordan's Bay. Predictably, both of them were up and at it around 5 a.m. Each went his way as they tackled some minor chores. Both of them were back at Little Mora before 7 a.m. and ready to have some fried eggs with a couple of pieces of bacon and fish for breakfast with Grandpa. Grandpa informed them at breakfast he was heading into town and planned to pick up some milk, butter, and other miscellaneous supplies for them and the resort. Grandpa did not offer an invitation to Coy or Growler this time to come along and as was the case with this family, he also needed some alone time.

The three of them finished up breakfast, and Coy and Growler efficiently worked together cleaning up the dishes and straightening up the cabin. Grandpa grabbed his old cowboy hat off the hook to the left side of the door and put it on as he was stepping out of the cabin. He turned around and told them what he had planned and that he would be back some time before noon. He also told them to keep an eye out for new patrons, as there would be three cabin change-outs later in the day. Coy and Growler both nonverbally acknowledged together.

Coy said, "Drive safe, Grandpa, and have a nice time, and oh yeah, take it easy."

Grandpa chuckled as he stepped out of the cabin.

Coy and Growler finished up the chores and stepped out of the cabin. They both knew that any new arrivals would most likely show up after lunch. They also knew that time went fast, and they had better get out on the lake and catch a few. Coy knew the time ahead was for much more than fishing, and his anticipation antenna were on high alert.

"I am going to make one more quick check at the fish house. Would you please grab some worms and some leeches from the ice box? Let's meet down at the dock in about twenty minutes or so. Does that work?" Coy spoke in Growler's direction, knowing the response would be a raised eyebrow or a grunt, but he knew Growler would understand and comply.

It was now a little before 8 in the morning. They met up at Dock 1, and it was time for them to make their way out to Jordan's Bay. Coy once again became the captain of the boat by running the motor and guiding it. He was feeling anxious, as he knew they would have to work together and guide the boat through the narrow strait entrance into Jordan's Bay. The weed beds were maturing more each day. Coy remembered the last time he jumped off the dock; it appeared the water was lower on the dock. The rocks between the main body of water of the lake and the bay were treacherous to get through in the early spring but as summer seasoned, the pathway became harder to find and work his way through.

The day was awakening with the sun high enough to pierce down some respectable heat. There was a light breeze, and the waves were a bit choppy on the main body of water. Coy anticipated the waves would be very slight within the Jordan's Bay as usual. Since it was still morning, the sun shined all the way to the west shoreline, and there would be a glare when looking into the bay. There were no cabins or evidence of civilization anywhere around the small bay, which was the size of a round forty-acre field. It was sometimes hard to estimate distances with no perspectives for balance, especially while going through the narrow passageway.

Jordan's Bay was on the southwest corner of the 320-acre lake. The lake water flowed from the river-fed zone somewhere near the radio tower northeast shoreline and the undercurrent of river-fed water flowed through Lake Esquagamah right through Jordan's Bay and out the small creek and culvert under the gravel road. Grandpa told Coy the water eventually made its way back to the Mississippi River a few miles south. It amazed Coy how the living water of the river knew where to go while feeding the lake with a beautiful, wonderful supply of fish. The lake was named after an Indian tradition, and it was without a doubt the river that brought the Indians to the lake.

Coy thought about how Growler would have to shut the motor down and row his way into Jordan's Bay when he was out there alone. Grandpa told Coy he would have to do the same if Coy ever wanted to enter the narrow strait alone. While Grandpa told Coy the instructions, he recited, "Row, Row, Row your boat gently down the stream, merrily, merrily, merrily, life is but a dream."

They were now out in the main body of the lake and heading to the entrance of Jordan's Bay. The sounds and feelings of a summer day out on the lake were always resplendent in the morning with the light waves' banging sounds on the side of the boat along with the hum of the motor. Birds were whistling their songs and communication abounded. Almost every time out on the lake, there would be two loons singing periodically back and forth to each other with their beautiful haunting sound, communicating to the world and each other.

Coy had thoughts of trepidation about going through the narrow gateway that led to Jordan's Bay. However, for some unknown reason he felt comfort knowing he and Growler would handle the task together. He considered the depth of water might be lower than the last time he went in the bay with Grandpa. Typically, folks would shut the motor down and raise it up and row through the small, meandering, lily pad-infested opening. The opening was only about forty or fifty yards, but boaters needed to be careful to stay on course because the water would become quite shallow to maybe two or three feet.

They approached the thick weeded area and found the entrance and started making their way through the narrow passageway. Growler got up on his knees on the front seat of the boat, and Coy raised the motor two notches so the propeller was just barely in the water. Growler, with hand signals, expertly guided Coy and the boat, and they made it through without incident or verbal communication into Jordan's Bay. Once in the bay, Coy could not help but think he would not be able to make it into Jordan's Bay without Growler's guidance.

One of the enduring qualities Growler liked about Coy was how this young man of twelve would fall into the trap of oversimplification, and he was so very free from the common prejudices that could block out acceptance of situations and realities. They worked together and made their way into Jordan's Bay with ease and handled the task with simplicity. It was natural for Growler to move into position as they worked together to make a bigger task smaller and more manageable. Growler yearned to simplify his life and now when he saw it in practice, valued it.

By early July, the weed undergrowth and exposed lily pads would grow thick and entangled anything brave enough to venture in its path. As spring grew into summer, the entrance into Jordan's Bay would gradually become more overgrown to a point of being hard to even identify. They made their way into the bay, and Coy was reminded of when one of those big northern pike fish had no choice but to attempt to swim right through the mesh of a large landing net. Once caught up in the weeds or net, the first thought would be to grab a handful of throttle when the best choice very well could be something different.

They drifted peacefully into the bay. Coy grabbed a handful of throttle for a few seconds and then shut the throttle down to a slow trolling speed so they could move into position near the west shoreline. Growler pointed out the location for a decent fishing area, just outside but still within the confines of the lily pads on the west shoreline. Growler had a specific location in mind. He pointed toward the southwest shoreline, which was where he would position himself and the boat on Sunday mornings. Growler looked at Coy frequently and guided the young captain with hand gestures and a few grunts. He held the anchor by its rope flopping at his side as he hoisted it right above the water, ready to drop it at just the right location. Coy enjoyed the teamwork and took a deep breath. He felt like time was at a standstill.

Yearning eagerness filled Coy's heart, but he did not want to show it in any way.

Growler guided Coy to his specific location and when ready, dropped the anchor and tied it off. He looked back at Coy and then looked around. He stopped and stared directly at the white building up on the top of the hill on the south shoreline. He turned toward Coy and nodded downward slowly. Coy knew they were at the right spot.

Coy looked around the boat and prepared to fish. He examined the shoreline, the water, and weeds around them to figure out where he thought would be a good spot to wet his line. He had his fishing pole in his hand, and he was also mentally preparing to ask his wave of questions. Then Growler spoke, anticipating Coy's thoughts.

"We are like the ducks and geese, Coy, seeking some clear water upon which to rest ourselves and to obtain an easy existence." He paused for a moment and continued. "The problem is if we imitate the ducks and geese, we follow guides that have no forethought for if they or we had any, they would not settle on clear water where they can be seen by an eagle, who would catch them easily."

Growler's statement and communication froze time. Coy had no idea how to respond or even if he should respond, so he went into a memory trance of thought. Coy was in learning mode and, unfortunately, this morning, it all flew right past him like hummingbirds in a hurry. Coy usually tried to take it in a bit before he started with his questions, but he had no idea how to respond or how to start asking questions. Coy pondered the comments and pieces of wisdom that bounced off him like a dropped football. He realized he could barely remember getting out of bed this morning as it seemed like days ago. His mind was everywhere else and right there at the same time. Nonetheless, for some funny reason, he did remember what Growler said about the birds.

As the waves relaxed down from and around the boat, they settled into the exact position Growler directed them to and desired. Coy looked around and up at the sky and realized this was a wonderful summer Sunday morning in July 1973 in northern Minnesota. He had been out on the lake a few times to fish during the previous couple of weeks with Grandpa and Growler. But he really looked forward to and was ready to enjoy this time with Growler out on the boat on the lake all alone for much more than fishing. Coy was hoping this would become a typical occurrence and destination on Sunday mornings for the two friends for the next couple of weeks until it was time to part. It saddened Coy to think he only had a possibility to have a few more Sundays with Growler out on Jordan's Bay.

Sunday mornings became Coy's most anticipated time of the week. He calculated he would be at the resort for thirty-four days from the time he was dropped off and that meant, he would have a total of five Sundays alone with Growler to communicate verbally all the questions of the world. He had been at the resort for a few weeks, and he realized he only had two or maybe three potential Sunday mornings to be with Growler alone out in Jordan's Bay. The first couple of weeks Growler went out to the bay alone, and Coy was very pleased to be his guest now.

Coy had mentally prepared all week and pondered questions and rehearsed them out loud during his alone time. He practiced in an attempt to be smoother and braver with the questions he wanted desperately to ask. He wanted to learn so much about this man and this morning the first question, which had been rehearsed for a few days, was ready to be asked.

Coy awakened from his memory trance. They were both fishing and catching fish and picking up a few keepers now and then. Coy did not even think or even know if he could or had to respond to Growler. "You know Growler..." He spoke up to the space between them anyway. He hesitated with unease and continued, "Does absence make the heart grow fonder?"

Coy wished he would have been able to come up with a more appropriate question or an important, momentous question. However, he learned the best way to learn and decipher this mystery would be by short and perhaps meek questions. He did not want to get off on roadways with tangled and messed up endings. Although this morning, it was time to ask the brave questions. He remembered something his dad once told him, "You know what, son, sometimes it only takes a few brave seconds of guts to be really, really brave."

The story and mystery of Growler was being painted right in front of him in the past couple of weeks and even though the colors and landscapes were as unclear as the murky Esquagamah lake water, he suspected he could still window shop for the fish below the water surface like fishing right next to the boat where he could see the fish taking and nibbling at the bait.

It seemed all thoughts were growing and becoming new to Coy. He had been in the bay before with Grandpa when they took out the Dock 3 boat and tested the three-horse Johnson to make sure it was running and ready for the guests. Grandpa wanted to show Coy Jordan's Bay and, more importantly, the process of entry into the bay. Coy did the guiding on that day, and Grandpa ran the motor.

Coy was always enamored and outright amazed with Grandpa when they shared new experiences. Grandpa, being in his late seventies and a little bit crippled up, was vibrant and easily handled the boat and motor. Coy helped guide the boat through the narrow way on his knees on the front bench of the boat while simultaneously watching the water and keeping a careful eye on Grandpa's every move. Coy, even when he was younger, could tell just about everything and all the intricacies his grandpa possessed, starting with facial movements and vocal inflections. Coy knew how to get into Jordan's Bay, and he knew he needed help and guidance.

Growler went out to Jordan's Bay every Sunday morning, and this was the first time he was willing to be out there with a guest. Coy had been taught many times from his mother that if he was an invited guest, he should be a good guest.

Growler did not answer Coy's question but responded with, "Young man, Thomas Wolfe keeps whispering in my head."

Up until this point there was no back-and-forth verbal answers to questions, just statements. It was as if they were out there talking to themselves and the air like two people walking in different directions, wanting to be together. Coy suspected his question/statement might just permeate the rest of their conversation.

Often, the western shoreline was a place of serenity. The trees would overhang, and the sunlight would hit the water about twenty feet from shore right where the lily pads began. The sensation of wind was the pleasant sound of the ruffling leaves high in the trees. The water's surface was calm and had a soft feeling that coincided with Coy feeling mushy inside his belly. The shoreline this morning was peaceful and there were little to no waves in the water. However, the real worldly noise came from the buzz of flies, flapping of wings, and chirping of the birds living and surviving.

Coy hesitated to embrace a theory he had not tested in his own young experience, something his mom called patience. The desire for answers and truth clutched upon his thoughts like clouds clutching the wrong side of the rays of sunlight. They fell upon Coy's revelations moment by moment with Growler with no moving obstacles. Coy wanted every bit of communication to be like the light of the day, which became brighter as the day grew. The colors in the trees on the shoreline became clearer and more beautiful as Coy gazed at them with vigor, hoping the distraction would help him break into the barrier called Growler.

Growler was looking up at the white building, which was at least forty feet up from the south shoreline and up a steep hill. There was a wooden stairway that began at a small dock where a small row boat was attached. They were fifty feet or so from the dock and the water was four to five feet deep where they were fishing. Coy looked the same direction as Growler and then closely at the stairway. He could not see the construction of the stairs and he wondered how they could possibly have been built on such a steep slope. Coy's first thought was that the desire to have an entrance to the white building on top of the stairway must have been very important.

Coy looked in all directions to get his bearing and spotted the small creek some forty feet to the northwest. This was the creek crossing under a culvert a mile or so down the road from the white building.

Coy broke the silence and distractions. "Why here, and why this time, Growler?" He spoke quietly as if just to himself, and he hoped Growler had not heard him. Then, he asked, "Why Thomas Wolfe?"

Growler turned his head and looked right at Coy and lifted his left eyebrow. A signature move of acceptance and maybe amazement that the young man actually heard the few comments he put out in the world.

"This is a good fishing spot and not too far off the under-river flow, young man. We should easily catch a few," Growler responded.

"Oh, that God allow it," was Growler's second response.

Though young and naive, Coy had an innate ability to recognize when it just was time to push the subject.

Coy simply responded, "You are right again." The boat rocked from the slight breeze in the air and the waves, Coy's response fit the fishing spot comment, but of course he wanted more.

Growler eyes and heart were fixed on the white building on top of the hill, as if he wanted to be somewhere else on these Sunday mornings. The fishing was always secondary to something else, especially because it was very easy to catch fish at just about any location on the western shoreline in Jordan's Bay.

Growler turned back around and kept looking up at the white building, as if searching for something or hoping for answers. Coy looked at Growler and then turned his body around to fish out of the back of the boat. He also could look at the stairs and the white building right on cue. Coy's purpose was the answers and stories. He thoroughly enjoyed Growler's voice and was overwhelmed by the history and information shared whenever they were together.

Coy turned slightly in position and discerned the white building had a small bell tower sprouting from its roof. At

9:30 on Sunday mornings, the bells went off and continued every fifteen minutes, but rang with extra vigor at exactly ten o'clock. The sound of the bells ringing could be heard as far away as the resort although, it would be muddled with a slight echo. The echo sound from the bells was clear from Jordan's Bay, and was loud enough to cause slight tremors on the water surface. Even the fish would be awakened and had to know the time must be special. Coy enjoyed the exact poignant moment each Sunday morning. After the bells reverberated through the air, everyone's listening skills would heighten with the anticipation. Coy could hear the loons from the main lake area and the wild sound of geese cries, yet nothing was as beautiful as those bells, and nothing was as special as the look on Growler's face as he would carefully sit and listen. The sound of the 9:30 bells stopped and Coy took his time and asked again so Growler would hear.

"Why now and why here, Growler? Why?" "Because I love him," Growler said.

"You love who?" Coy asked.

"I love him because I know that he loves me," Growler went on.

Coy, a little confused, said, "Who loves who?"

Growler sat silently for what seemed like another eternity to Coy. It was maybe five minutes. The silence was broken with a raised eyebrow look, but this time with words also. Growler looked at Coy and said, "In time, young man and shortly, I will be brave enough to show you more. I remember reading a fine book when I was about your age written by Thomas Wolfe called, *You Can't Go Home Again*. He was so right! Life fills time with an illusion of prosperity, and time passing by relentlessly is so unfair. And, that is what prevents us all from ever being able to return home again." He stopped again. Coy sat and listened carefully, waiting for more.

"Please, I pray for you, Coy. Choose and understand that your life is not enough, because one lifetime is not enough! Life is too important not to live." Growler stopped as he was fishing and pulled in a nice keeper. "Absence does not make the heart grow fonder." He pulled the hook out of the fish he had just pulled into the boat and concluded by answering Coy's first question.

Coy was flabbergasted and taken aback that his first question was answered. The world went silent and both of them left the moment to enter their own time and thoughts.

CHAPTER 24

Part 2 Ten Years Later - The Beginning

The moment in time happened midday on the twelfth day of July 1983. The timing was almost ten years to the day when Coy first thought that he believed in Jesus Christ.

Coy was with his beautiful wife, the love of his life. They were sitting silently and closely on the small couch, holding hands, and both of them filled with emotions of fear, joy, love, and anticipation. There was a startling knock on the door of the small one-bedroom efficiency apartment, which was the upstairs of the 1919-built two-story home in North Minneapolis, Minnesota. According to the doctor's instructions, this was the day. They were only a few hours away from the trek to the hospital, as she was very close to giving birth to their first child. Coy stayed home from work this day to make sure to be there and ready when the time arrived. The knock on the door startled them like a rock dropped from the sky, disturbing a serene small pond of water.

They did not get many visitors. After the initial startle, Coy stood up and walked to the door and looked out the small window. It was the postman. Coy opened the door, and they exchanged pleasantries. The package being delivered was a bit too big to fit in the small mail slot in the mailbox mounted on the house at the bottom of the thirteen-step stairway outside. The package was marked 'VERY IMPORTANT'. The dutiful postman wanted to make sure that a package marked with importance was not missed by the recipient. He didn't feel comfortable leaving it at the bottom of the stairs as most good servants would have done. He wanted to make sure it was accepted and received, and he graciously made the extra effort to make sure the package was personally accepted.

Coy thanked the postman as he pensively looked at the package. The address and zip code were unfamiliar. However, he thought he recognized the town it came from, somewhere in Northern Minnesota. However, acting out the kid inside himself, he shook the package and went about opening it like a kid on Christmas morning.

The mystery package was formally addressed and wrapped with grocery bag paper and neatly tied with a small piece of twine. Once he removed the paper, he found a well-worn book wrapped securely with a large rubber band to keep the loose pages from slipping out. He immediately felt a presence from the past within an unknown, mysterious, yet memorable world. Nevertheless, he gathered himself and pulled the rubber band away from the book with consternation. He positioned it between his thumb and index finger on his left hand, softly pulled it back like a trigger, and shot at his wife's behind as she walked back to the couch in the living area. Once a kid, always a kid.

They laughed and giggled simultaneously. The little game helped cool down the tension in the air. They had been praying together five minutes earlier for patience, guidance, and hope.

They were scared and apprehensive, as their baby was due any moment. They were praying for a sign or something or a package from God, and this package was delivered.

The young, expectant mother looked back at Coy with a concerned awkward grin, discerning his consternation, and went to him. They hugged as they went down to their knees. He opened the package and recognized the book. He put the book under his arm and unfolded the one-page letter that was taped to the cover of the book and started to read it to himself.

"What is it honey, what is it? It's bad, isn't it?" she said with a frightened tone, while she backed off from their hug.

"It is a book. Well, kind of," he responded, as tears started falling like a drenching spring rain. A revelation was being exposed.

"What? What? From whom?" She moved to comfort and support her husband and wrapped her arms around his neck. "Whatever it is, we will get through it, honey." She softly spoke as she gave him a light kiss on his cheek.

Coy did not speak. He was in faraway place where time and space were frozen.

He softly emerged from his zone and read out loud the brief letter.

> *Mr. C. J. Storeslight during the last week of his life, with help, wrote a few letters of information along with instructions to send this book to you. The hospital staff made sure to get the information and final instructions to us at the Church.*
>
> *We are reaching out to you as there were specific instructions with favor for you to attend his memorial service and speak on his behalf, even if you were the only one to attend.*

Please attend. The instructions say that you will know the location of the church.

Praise God.

The service is on Sunday morning, July 17, 1983, at 10 a.m.

Sincerely with God's blessing,

Pastor J.

His young wife turned his head towards her and gave him a loving kiss. She knew and understood. They hugged dearly.

Their baby boy was born at 11:22 p.m. on July 12, 1983. Coy and his dear wife closely hugged each other as they held their son together. Even in the presence of what was a life-changing surreal moment, all Coy could think about was another life, one particular life. "Please, God," he prayed silently to himself as his wife was leaning in, "let this boy grow among the best of them with You in his heart and with an open and childlike way for life forever and according to Your will, because one lifetime is not enough."

Mother and baby all came through it splendidly and within two days, they were back in their small apartment. A home where there once was two, now there were three. None of them slept much for the next couple of days. Coy helped where he could with his wife and son, all while carefully studying the book and untangling his memory.

Coy woke up at his usual time five days later, at around 5:00 a.m., and went out for a brisk morning walk, which really doubled as a wakeup call for his body as well as his alone time for thought and meditation. This morning he used the time for his final preparation. He loved the early morning freshness of air, a quality he had obtained and learned years before at the Lake Esquagamah resort.

They decided together that Coy would take some days off from work to help around the house after the baby arrived, but he had to admit he really was not much help. He spent every moment during those five days helping just enough to keep his wife happy and try to give her momentary breaks from early motherhood while his mind was in wonderment between becoming a father to a son and the book.

Together, they decided that Coy would go to the funeral alone, as it was a little quick to be bringing a newborn on a road trip. They both had feelings of trepidation and nevertheless, prudence overruled and helped make the decision.

Most of his energy during the five days prior to jumping in his 1972 step side Chevy pickup and making the two-and-a-half-hour road trip to the church that the note said he would know was invested in reading through the book he had not seen in ten years. Many times, he went into his memory, thinking about the book and the writing down of clear thoughts he had read from ten years past. He remembered reciting phrases and thoughts time and time again during his formative teenage years. Coy always felt the book he read from years before could have been a description of a man's life or something like a Bible. He analyzed the handwritten notes and small sheets of loose note paper with dates, times, and names of people. He kept coming to sections of the book he remembered, which kept him even more interested as the mystery was being revealed. He was yearning to have further understanding of the mystery and get answers to questions that haunted him occasionally during the downtimes from the pressures of his adult life. He had concluded that some mysteries might remain mysteries for a reason.

Coy power-read through the book twice, as he wanted to permanently etch the words in his mind. He realized he had not asked for any help and on day two of his preparation decided that he should be praying for answers and guidance for enlightenment and blessing. He set down the book on the couch, went to their bedroom, and grabbed his Bible, which he kept on the shelf of the nightstand along with his memoir book. Coy opened his worn personal Bible with all its notes and loose papers and asked God for guidance, and it was provided. From that time on, Coy would always end his praying time with: "And Your will be done, because one life *is* not enough, according to Your pleasure, dear Lord." Answers were being given and received.

CHAPTER 25

The Moment in Time Was Now

C oy was already back from his early walk on the morning of July 17, 1983.

His wife and newborn son were peacefully sleeping in the bedroom. He quietly prepared a couple pieces of toast and grabbed a few pieces of fish fillet out of the refrigerator left over from the night before. He sat down on the couch, said a prayer of thanksgiving for all God had given him, and ate his breakfast.

By the time he finished eating and cleaning up, his family was awake. He was happy he didn't have to wake them because it was time for him to make his trek to the memorial service, and he wanted to say goodbye. His wife followed him as he made his way through the door and stood on the top of the stairs outside their small apartment. The landing was part of an externally mounted steel stairway of thirteen steps down to the sidewalk. His young wife, with their baby in her arms, stepped out onto the landing. Coy gave his wife a loving kiss and hugged her as if it would be the last time to say goodbye and hug again. She was holding their son, and their baby boy was squeezed between them. She stepped back and handed the boy to him. Coy gave a loving hug and planted kisses with the same exuberance to their son. He felt a love he never felt before. This was a new life. This was a person he had something to do with, and an immense weight of responsibility fell upon his shoulders every time he looked at his wife and son. He felt part of the process of being born again. Where once there were two, now there were three and he loved every bit of it and knew life would never be the same. He had no idea why he liked it. Coy's love for his wife and son are without an ending.

He stepped down the stairway and as he stepped off onto the sidewalk, he looked up at them. To him, it was a picturesque view of a stairway with direct access to heaven. A wonderful view. His mind was swimming with past memories as it reminded him of looking up a stairway out on Jordan's Bay many years before. This time he felt a direct picturesque glimpse of heaven. "Goodbye, Teresa. Goodbye, Nicholas." He spoke quietly to himself while walking to his pickup truck. Good goodbyes could be timeless.

Coy sat down behind the wheel and placed his small carry-on bag that had his notes, the book, and personal Bible on the passenger side of the bench seat. He estimated the mileage and time it would take to get to the church. He did not want to be in a rush and wanted to absorb the whole experience of the journey. There was no question where that church was located. He wanted to feel and enjoy the whole experience as if he was twelve again. He drove up all the old roads and stayed off the freeway, driving through the towns that would have been the exact trek his family would have driven when he was younger. While keeping a close eye on the road, he tried to count the fence posts just like he would have with Sparky, their family dog in his lap, when his family headed up to the lake. The last time he came home from the lake, he did not have to count any fence posts.

Around 8 or half past 8 o'clock on the morning of July 17th, 1983, Coy turned the steering wheel of his pickup truck at what he remembered to be Robinson's Corner off Highway 169. The old Robinson building was gone, and now there was a new convenience store with gas pumps. The name on the sign right at the corner was 'Claire Bear.' He pulled in there briefly to look the place over, and he noticed the sign below the door which read, 'Where spunk meets the road.' Coy pulled out of the lot and was now driving on the old gravel road to Lake Esquagamah. He noticed the sign on the road was Claire Road, which was a new name, but it was the same old beat-up road. He knew he was only a couple of miles to the destination. He slowed down to ten or fifteen miles per hour on the gravel road, as he wanted to be that young Coy again who lived and felt the anticipation of seeing the lake for the first time. His eagerness for seeing the lake had never left his memory.

He drove right past the small white church building and down the hill to see the old resort. He had not been up there for ten years. He only had a picture in his mind of how it must have changed and grown in the world. He rolled down the hill slowly in anticipation and looked for the small resort entrance road and found it easily. As he looked up to find Little Mora, the cabins, people, boats, motors, and everything about the resort, he realized the resort was gone. Coy had heard through the family grapevine that the resort had been torn down and things changed up at Lake Esquagamah. He did not want to believe it and once again, outward appearances confirmed the story. He never wanted to admit it or even think that the whole resort was gone, dead.

A glimpse of a memory came back to him as he remembered what his Uncle Hilb told him once while they cleaned fish together in the old fish house one summer evening. "Coy, often we learn when you go back somewhere important in your past and where you had not been at in a while, you will notice how much the trees and life grow around memories." Coy was stopped in his track as this was a complete change. The trees and life had not just grown around his memories. All that was left was the memory.

A new house was built close to the spot where the old shed had been, built with a style that appeared to give the whole area a look of rebirth. There was new siding, roof, and windows. The landscaping and the lawn were immaculate, which was very pleasant to Coy. But as he turned onto the old resort entrance road, he realized he surely was not that twelve-year-old Coy anymore. He looked at the house and suspected no one was home, as it seemed silent and there were no vehicles around.

He stopped his truck right at the old entrance to the resort, which had become nothing more than the driveway to a new home. The small landing road no longer ended at the lake, as it was designed as an entrance and exit for the people who lived in the house. The one pleasant caveat was that the whole scene was serene. The trees were groomed neatly, a freshly cut lawn covered where there once were cabins and life was once lived. To Coy, an unbelievably neatly groomed landscape and a beautiful lawn went right up and around Chelsea Brook with neatly built crossover walking bridges. The lake looked about the same, as he could now see the whole shoreline from the road with no blockage of view caused by cabins or people and life.

Coy parked and turned off the pickup truck and opened the door and stepped out of the vehicle. He decided to walk around and try to get a feel. He wanted to be very prepared this morning and felt his final preparation must start with being in the presence of something, although he had no idea how or any knowledge of what it could be.

He walked the estimated number of steps from the resort entrance to the east to find the Little Mora Cabin location and as he walked, he felt his grandpa walking right beside him. He walked to each of the cabin locations and remembered the people he had befriended. He walked and let his mind flow with past memories. He wanted the Lord to stop him and give him some thoughts and peace when the time was right.

After roaming around for about fifteen minutes, he stopped, looked around, and found a fallen, bent over tree. He realized it was the tree where the tire swing was hung. It had fallen towards the road lying on its side and had not yet been cut off, obviously still alive and dead at the same time. Coy quickly calculated the appropriate distance from the tree to where the fish house would have been and sat down on the trunk right where the fish house would have been. As silly as he thought he was acting, he looked around like he was in the fish house with Growler and took a deep breath of air, hoping to catch a smell from the fish guts pail.

He carefully grabbed the book he had put in his coat pocket. He thought this would be the best place in the world for his final preparation. He mumbled a short prayer and asked God to open the book to the exact location where he should finalize his thoughts and, most importantly, ease his mind.

He opened the book and as he had deciphered over the past few days, there were several locations within the book where there were recitations and the words written down from Bible passages, always in the King James Version. His forefinger landed on a title: 1 Corinthians, chapter 15. The first four verses had been marked, and a small note was written on the side in capital letters: *THIS IS THE GOSPEL.*

Coy commenced to speak out loud as he read:

> "Moreover, brethren, I declare unto you the gospel which I preached unto you, which also ye have received, and wherein ye stand; By which also ye are saved, if ye keep in memory what I preached unto you, unless ye have believed in vain. For I delivered unto you first that which I also received, how that Christ died for our sins according to the scriptures; And that he was buried, and that he rose again the third day according to the scriptures."

He stopped, bowed his head, and knew a glimpse of Christ was all that was needed and just maybe, Growler was the glimpse needed and at just the right time in his life.

Coy continued reading out loud. "A prophet is a messenger from God, the word in Hebrew meaning 'one who speaks for another.' He can be rich or destitute, educated or unlearned, from noble ranks or the fields." At that moment, Coy had an epiphany and he thought perhaps a twenty-two-year-old kid from Minneapolis, Minnesota, might fit the bill even though not worthy or ready. This morning and forever more, Coy realized it was time to accept that one lifetime was enough.

CHAPTER 26

Don't Count Your Time. Make Your Time Count

Twenty minutes or so into reading and reciting, Coy remembered that he needed to pray and ask God for His hand of guidance. He continued on for a few more minutes and decided it was time to make his way back to his pickup, as it was now around 9:15 a.m. He got up from the tree and walked back to his pickup, jumped in, started it up, turned it around, and left the resort area. He made the right-hand turn and drove up the hill the thousand feet or so to the entrance to the church. As he made the turn into the parking lot of the white building on top of the hill, which he always knew was a church, he felt the past come alive as if he was still hiding in the ditch looking for answers. Suddenly an echo of memory went off, and he remembered his old football coach from the past say, "Boys, this team will live according to Vince Lombardi time, and we will abide by this rule: fifteen minutes early you are on time, fifteen minutes late and you will be forgotten." Coy made a vow the day he heard this wisdom and continued to live with that premise. On this extraordinary morning, he wanted to live on double Lombardi time, so he felt forty-five minutes prior to the service would be proper.

The inviting sign on the road read: *Welcome to the church on the on top of the hill on the other side of Jordan's Bay—JORDAN'S Baptist Church.*

He thought the church was fittingly named. However, he remembered it as Hilltop Church, or something like that. Even the name of the church had changed.

Coy slowly pulled into the parking area and saw there were only a couple of vehicles. He decided to park on the northwest side of the lot where he would be far enough to the side and where he could possibly be able to look over Lake Esquagamah. He parked the pickup, sat there in solemn silence, and leaned on the steering wheel as he turned off the engine. His curiosity was on high alert, just as if he was in detective mode again and a twelve-year-old. He carefully looked around the surroundings from behind the wheel. It took less than ten seconds when his thoughts of his dear wife and son entered his mind. That was right when he knew he was not that twelve-year-old anymore. However, it did remind him that the twelve-year old was still present. His first impressions came from the dusty leaves of the vibrant summer life of the trees that surrounded the church parking lot. The leaves hung on the tree as if they were gray and lifeless, even though they had color. However, the morning sun was just reaching the top of the trees, which he remembered would bring the color and life to everything.

He looked over Lake Esquagamah toward the west shore and remembered those clear summer evenings when the rays of the setting sun shined across the highest peaks of the tallest trees on the shoreline with pink and gold hue. It would give him and everyone discernment hope. The color of the trees and leaves surrounding the church came back to life as the sun shone down and became vibrant right before his eyes. He remembered those Sunday mornings on Jordan's Bay with Growler and how the sounds of life and fresh morning air would pour down life on them with a radiant glow.

He broke away from his thoughts while sitting behind the wheel and began to realize history and thoughts might never be complete, so he decided to take a walk and walk around and do a once-over stroll to help clear his mind. He opened the door to his pickup quietly and gently stepped out as if he was afraid someone might notice him or hear him. He wanted to walk around and take a look at the ambiance of the entire setting and look over the church building as well as the beautiful view over Jordan's Bay and Lake Esquagamah from on top of the hill and check to see if the stairway was still there. He immediately walked over to the steep shoreline and looked over Lake Esquagamah. He turned around and, for the first time, looked at the church from the north side and not from Jordan's Bay, as he had only seen this side of the church from the bay in a small fishing boat. It was well maintained, and he thought the building must have grown, as it looked so much bigger up close. He thought life was the same way: it looked so much bigger when he was looking closely. The stairway was there and a small boat was attached to the dock. There were no boats in Jordan's Bay, but he could hear an outboard motor coming from the direction of the main body of the lake to the west. He realized the church was almost directly west of the narrow passageway of the main body of water and above the southwest shoreline of Jordan's Bay.

Coy was thinking and walking with confidence even though an event of some solemnity and importance was going to take place. His experience and past voice were speaking loudly into his young adult mind and he knew this place and felt comfort. He was wondering if this morning the mourners would be gathered who would empathize with the homelessness or the mysteriousness of the deceased. Coy knew there was so much more. He knew the deceased extolled in hyperbole something that suggested a life far out of the ordinary. He could feel from deep within his soul the faith, hope, and love. Coy's heart pinged with a lonely hope to help share understanding.

He turned around again and looked over Lake Esquagamah. He spotted the radio tower on the far north shore of the main body of water, over the top of the tree line. He went back in memory and could see himself with Growler on those Sunday mornings out on Jordan's Bay.

Coy shook his head and tried to remember some of the history after he left the resort that late summer day from ten years in his past. He remembered Uncle Hilb telling him some information at a family picnic a couple of years after he had been at the resort.

Martha died the spring of '74. The resort died in '75. Grandpa died in the spring of '79. The summer of '74 did not work for Coy to spend time at the resort. He went to a Bible camp for a week, a wrestling camp for another week, and then baseball camp. By early August, football practice started and he never went back up to Lake Esquagamah that summer or ever again before the resort was demolished. In the spring of '75, the last of the cabins were demolished, and the land was cleared for neatly cut grass with a few empty potential campsites. There was no lake access, no fish house, no cabins, and no one, only history and memories. New life did go on and the old life disappeared. He remembered once again how he just did not want to believe all had changed, and the resort was gone.

He walked around to the entrance area of the church and, once again, became very impressed by the upkeep and landscaping. He stepped to the front door area and was startled as a man opened the door right when he stepped in front of it. Coy estimated the man to be in his early forties. He stepped out from behind the door to greet Coy without hesitation. They stood together in front of the entrance of the church. Coy was startled, yet he felt it could have been ten years earlier as he watched this same action from the ditch while a young man greeted Growler. They warmly shook hands, and Coy looked him in the eyes and believed he recognized and knew the man.

"I have been watching all morning for you. I saw you, through my office window, the second you pulled in the parking area. I am the pastor here. I just knew it had to be you. Once I saw you walking, I knew it was you. You walk with such purpose and on your tiptoes as if the next step is always important. Somehow, I knew that to be a quality you would have. I imagined you would do a quick look around and now, you are here. Do you remember me or know me?"

The pastor welcomed and guided Coy through the church front door.

"Yes, I do, I think." Coy answered timidly. "Thank you for finding me, I do not know how you did it, but thank you very much, and God bless you!" Coy spoke up in his normal tone and diction.

"God bless you, my friend. Our Father in heaven wants you here," the pastor conveyed with a kind undertone.

"I really want to be here," Coy responded.

"Thank God! It is such a blessing when one wants to be right where God wants us to be," the pastor replied. "It is very nice that you are early. I am not sure how many people will be here this morning, but we sent out quite a few notices through our small congregation and put information in the local papers all the way to Duluth. Please, let's step into my office for a few minutes, where we can pray together and prepare our hearts," the pastor said with a caring, soft tone.

"Thank you, Pastor," Coy responded with a heartfelt tone. Coy followed the pastor into the office and realized he had never been inside the building before. The office was well decorated with a wall of shelves filled with books. Coy could not help but look at the full bookshelves with awe and delight.

"Isn't it strange what happens with old books? They choose you. A few years ago, an anonymous donor sent boxes filled with these precious books to our church. Books seem to reach out when needed and say—Hello, here I am, take me with you. It's as if they are alive," the pastor said, while Coy looked at the shelves full of books.

Coy could only respond with a timid, "Yes." He remembered looking at the envelope sent to him with Growlers book a week before and noticing that only the name of the church was noted and turned his attention to the pastor. He realized he did not know this man's real name, remembering the letter was signed by Pastor J.

However, before Coy could ask a question, the pastor asked, "Is Coy your full name, and do you have a full first name?" He sat down behind a neatly organized oak desk and invited Coy to sit in the comfortable leather armchair in front of the desk.

The pastor broke the ice with the first probing question in the solitude of a conversation between two bonded souls.

Each of them felt a little like they were being cut open like a couple of fish on the cleaning table with guts and blood poured out into the hands of the cleaner, but the helpless fish still had some life and moved around. Coy heard the question and with honor and respect. He wanted to give an appropriate response.

"My full name is Timothy Coy."

"You are Timothy?" the pastor responded with a slight smirk, yet with an enchanted look.

"Yes, why does it seem like you are delighted?" Coy continued.

"Oh, please forgive me if I seem awkward; I really am taken aback a bit but for some reason not surprised," the pastor said as he motioned again for Coy to have a seat.

"I, well, I will say I feel very blessed and I am very pleased that you are here today," the pastor continued.

As Coy sat down, he reached into his nicely trimmed and funeral appropriate suit coat and grabbed the book that had been sent to him.

"Obviously, you received the package. Are you ready to give some thoughts this morning?" the pastor asked.

"I am," Coy acknowledged.

"Great answer." The pastor chuckled, grabbed his handkerchief, rubbed his temple, and wiped a small tear from his right eye.

"Are you okay?" Coy asked.

"Oh, nothing. Please do not read anything into my actions, I sometimes show emotions very quickly," he said while he gave out a muffled snicker. "God Himself could not have answered that question better, Coy, oh, I mean Timothy."

Coy did not quite know how to respond. He was more in thought on how he was to correct his name information. He was known as Coy for his whole life thus far, but it was always in the back of his mind his real first name was Timothy.

Coy pondered for a moment, remembering how he ended up always known as Coy. His sister Debbie struggled right away with his name, as she was a bit less than two years old when he was born. Early on, she had become his spokesperson and his best friend. Coy was told often he did not have to talk until he was four or five. Debbie did all the communicating and talking for the both of them. She was his caretaker and cheerleader, and she loved him very much. She always called him Coy and once he did start talking and communicating verbally, he liked the name. All the family liked it, so he became Coy. Besides, he loved his sister very much, and she liked knowing she was responsible for giving him his name. He liked that she felt special, because she was.

"Well then." The pastor broke the thirty-second silence as both had been in different places for a few moments. "Are you ready? The service begins in about thirty minutes or so."

"Yes, I believe that I am... well, I tried really hard to prepare, and I hope and pray God will deliver for and through for us and, most importantly, for him," Coy responded with a little confidence.

"You are so right, Timothy. We do need to pray together before we go forward. We, at the church, are so pleased you are prepared and care. Mr. C. J. Storeslight's discernment and obvious admiration toward you and your life appears, as expected, to be right on," the pastor continued.

"What? I know we do not have much time, but did he talk with you about me, or did he talk to anyone or anything?" Coy asked.

"Oh no, no one ever heard a single word come out of his mouth, even though so many wanted him to talk and say something and give us some information or tell us something or just to help solve the wonder and mystery. He never spoke, but he communicated so generously in so many ways," the pastor responded.

"Wow, what?" was all Coy could say in response, and the pastor skipped right over that response.

"Well then, before we pray, it is time for me to share with you something we received in the paperwork from the hospital. It is a brief one-page instruction he wrote down and gave to the hospital staff the day before he passed. Let's pray somehow we can complete this puzzle." The pastor stopped speaking and reached into his Bible sitting on the right side of his desk, opened it, and took out a formal-looking envelope and one piece of paper. "This is for you, Coy. The note explicitly tells me to give this envelope to you to open the day of his memorial service. It also says the information in this envelope is specifically for you."

He handed Coy the note and the envelope. Coy was dumbfounded and speechless.

"That book you have in your hand appears to be the remaining material estate of this man. He really wanted you to have it. We were not only quite flabbergasted but very thankful for all his generosity. In the past ten years, his life touched so many hearts well beyond any life any of us have ever known. However, other than his writings and that book in your hand, he left this world with no gold, no silver, no land, no manuscripts, no works of art, and no position of authority or title from his life, as far as any of us knew. He gave away everything he had in the last ten years. For some reason beyond our understanding, he was especially kind and generous to this church family and to me personally and my family. But you would have known that already, I suppose.

He gave of his life to help others find life." The pastor stopped speaking, grabbed his handkerchief again, and wiped tears from both his eyes.

Coy sat there and listened to every word carefully while at the same time his heart was bursting with awe and excitement and joy.

"We have been overwhelmed with gratefulness over the years as somehow and some way, God provided for our family at just the right time every time. And to this day, we have no understanding of the gracious giving we received from this mysterious man."

The pastor stopped again and looked Coy right in the eyes. Coy looked intently back and saw eyes that people would take up the sword for and follow.

"We knew his health was starting to fail, and I went up several times in the last two months and prayed for and over him. He did not respond verbally to me ever, but his look was of pure thankfulness. We were made aware of his death by the hospital, and all he had on him was that book, his personal Bible, written instructions, an envelope addressed to me, and one for you addressed to the church. We, at the church, looked through his meager belongings and written notes and as we came across that book, we were overwhelmed in our discovery. When we found this information, we began to realize who he was, and we carefully followed the information with specific instructions to find you and get this book to you. When we paged through the book, we found this one envelope addressed to our church, which was wrapped around a sealed envelope I kept out before I sent the book off to you. On the back of the envelope, there is a hand-written note that I am to personally give this sealed envelope to you. We, at the church, cannot wait to see what is in this envelope."

As the pastor finished, he reached into his coat pocket and pulled out a piece of paper and the sealed envelope, all of which looked formal.

"His notes had specific instruction to show this to you right before the memorial service, if there was to even be a service. We, at this church, were in no way *not* going to have a memorial service for this dear man," the pastor said.

"Wow," was all Coy could muster.

The pastor handed Coy the sheet of paper and the sealed envelope and as he did, he stood up and walked around the desk and gave Coy a warm, loving, Christian hug. They broke from the hug.

The pastor said, "You will need a few minutes. Let us pray,"

They held each other's hands in harmony as they both in unison bowed their heads, and the pastor spoke out a prayer.

"Father God, thy will be done as it is in heaven, give us our daily provisions and forgive us our fleshly thoughts of life here on earth. As You told us, we forgive others. Give us Your will, and Your will be done." The pastor's short prayer said it all.

Coy felt the presence of God after their private bonding prayer. The pastor stepped out of the office to give Coy a few minutes to ponder and look over the information and to prepare his heart with final thoughts before the service.

Coy read the note and then looked over the envelope and opened it. He was staggered yet enlightened by what was written down on the top of this formal piece of paper that looked like a copy of a birth certificate. Coy prayed for God's guidance and was overwhelmed with the answer and responsibility before him.

After ten or fifteen minutes, he decided it was time. He said a short prayer for guidance and stepped out of the office. He came upon a few people gathered at the entrance to the sanctuary. There was a small picture of Growler in a nice frame on a miniature homemade easel at the entrance to the sanctuary. Coy looked and deduced the picture had been taken in the not so distant past and noticed how Growler had aged since he had seen him. He pondered thinking about what Growler must have looked like when he was in his thirties or forties and still quite vibrant and full of life at some faraway place in time. Growler had been cremated, and the small box container with his remains was of the simplest type and very likely built by someone at the church. Growler's ashes were placed on a small table centered at the front of the church. The small church comfortably held around eighty people. Coy glanced briefly into the sanctuary and looked directly at the small box placed on a table in front of the lectern. The ambience of the moment and scene with the container and picture was barely large enough to be a decent funeral, giving a very humble presence and feeling but to Coy, appropriate.

Coy continued to gather his thoughts in mental preparation, and he wandered around the back entrance welcome area outside the sanctuary. He looked out the window to the porte-cochere he now knew was held up by beams with a cross beam symbolizing 'The Cross.' It was the same cross from the other side he saw from the ditch years before. He hoped his comments would be lasting and appropriate as he thought about the obituary, he had found in the local Duluth newspaper. He had picked it up when he stopped in the town of Palisade for gas before coming out to the church. He was hoping there would be some nicely written obituary about Growler but, of course, he knew he would not find any, as no one really knew Growler. And, he also knew Growler was not his true name, so he perused over all the obituaries.

"In memory," wrote the author of one obituary, "we regret that we knew so little of the history of this distinguished stranger. The facts of his life were largely unknown and, apparently, he confided in no one…" Coy could not help but think it was about Growler, but then he realized that all people could be declared a mystery, depending on a point of view. It was an obituary of some former big rig mining executive from Hibbing, Minnesota.

Coy had ten years to find understanding, and thoughts of Growler and their experience together always brought him close to God and Christ. He remembered the facts of Growler's life were so hidden in his early life, where the seeds of a tragedy were much deeper than anyone could comprehend as if his life was lived in another world and spoken in another language. From afar, the impression was one of haunting loneliness, anonymity, and mystery. However, if anyone would have known the real Growler at all, it was Coy. At least, that was what he thought and hoped.

Coy felt the burden of the moment. He had to tell a truthful story – at least a glimpse.

CHAPTER 27

Back to the Dock, 1973

"Absence does not make the heart grow fonder." Growler ended his diatribe by answering Coy's first question.

Coy was flabbergasted and taken aback his first question was now answered. The world came back to life.

Growler and Coy had been out fishing in Jordan's Bay for almost two hours on Sunday morning, July 8, 1973, and it was around 11:30 a.m. Growler had talked for almost an hour without pause. He explained many details of his youth along with his immediate family background. Coy sat, listened, barely said a word, and acknowledged what he heard with nods and gestures. The fishing ended an hour earlier. Coy learned Growler was born in Thief River Falls, Minnesota, where his family and family farm was located. His family lived on a 120-acre farm, three miles southwest of Thief River Falls. They farmed around eighty acres of the land, pastured a small herd of cows, had a flock of twenty sheep and, of course, a brood of chickens. They lived in a small two-bedroom farmhouse with no running water or bathroom.

The land the farm was settled on was self-sustaining with a small fresh water supply, good ground water, and a dream location for hunting deer, grouse, partridge, squirrels, and rabbits. The land supplied the family well, but the old farm was never a money-maker. Growler told Coy during his youth, before he went in the service, he could not remember ever wearing new clothes or shoes.

On the day of his eighteenth birthday, he left and entered the service without hesitation or question and gave his youth a stoic goodbye. He quickly realized for the first time he was on a routine of three good solid meals a day, new clothes, boots, and life direction. Growler stated clearly that this point of time in his life was like entering a mini form of a new heaven.

Growler was born in 1917 right in one of the bedrooms of their home, the third of six children of three boys and three girls. Later in this life, he heard about the Roaring '20s, but never experienced any of the roar. He did experience the '30s, the Depression, and every bit of the tight survival life times. He had to grow up quickly and out of necessity, became self-sustaining like everyone else in the entire country outside of those who experienced the roar and, frankly, they did not know any different. The US Army was more than a break from past existence. He felt he entered a new and better life. Yet, he expressed kindhearted and good memories of his childhood and family. Nonetheless, being in the service was a boon. He liked the new clothes and boots and, more importantly, sustained purpose.

Growler told Coy his parents were direct immigrants from Germany with strong Protestant religious beliefs and that somehow and some way ended up in a small community in northeastern Minnesota. The entire community was filled with Catholics and Missouri Synod Lutherans. During his childhood, he never heard of music or festivity or anything separated from their religious beliefs and activities. Life was one. The family schedule revolved around church activities, such as family picnics, fishing and, most importantly, hunting. Hunting was the foundation of family bonding which ignited his impetus and strong overwhelming desire to excel at marksmanship. He wanted to go with the government when they picked him up on his eighteenth birthday. He welcomed it and looked forward to the challenge.

Growler emphasized time and time again during conversations with Coy that he wanted to find out why his thoughts were that one life was not enough. Life was always in transition from one location to another. Friends were transient. Family was trapped in memory.

He told Coy that when he was six or seven years old, he realized he was given one special gift from God and that was shooting a rifle and then a pistol and, frankly, any killing device he was asked to handle and overcome. Coy heard all about the background of his sharpshooting skills as a youth, winning contest upon contest. By the time he was twelve years old, everyone in the county knew about him. He won every state competition the family could get him to. The US Army came after him and started communicating with the family when he was fifteen years old. On his eighteenth birthday, the Army folks actually picked him up right at the farm, and his family and farm life was over.

Growler lived for the next six years until the beginning of the U.S. engagement in WWII not being able to contact or reach out to his family as he sharpened his skills with intense training. However, in the spring of 1941, at the age of twenty-four he was finally given his opportunity to go home. He was still the property of the United States government.

During the summer of 1941, he fell in love with a young lady along the way. He even had the opportunity to go to his family home in northeastern Minnesota to see them and the chance to make sure they would know he was still alive. Once there, he found all had changed. He found out his father had passed away, and his mother had lost the farm and was in the later stage of something they called senile dementia. He learned one of his brothers was living in Chicago selling insurance. The other brother lost his life in an automobile accident. His oldest sister was in St. Paul, married and happy with a couple of kids. His baby sister lived in Thief River Falls, worked at the hospital as a nurse and became the caretaker for their mother. He never actually saw any of them. He drove by the old homestead, and his memories were only exasperated with sorrow and loss, which was inevitable with a transient life.

Growler met his wife at his favorite restaurant one evening while having dinner alone during an Army training exercise near Kansas City, Missouri, the fall of 1940.

Tensions were on high alert in America with World War II going on in Europe. However, he had served his time, and it looked like his stretch with the Army might be coming to an end. Falling in love was not in the plans. But love happens, and they married and decided to move into a small apartment in Minneapolis, Minnesota, where he was planning on getting a job as a machinist or work at one of the mills along the Mississippi River near the Northside of Minneapolis. Their small apartment was right off Hennepin Avenue and 3rd Street, close to the booming mills. There were work opportunities in Minneapolis, and he was in love and ready to start a rewarding new life with his loving young wife. He told Coy how much he adored and loved his wife.

His voice would break up, and he stumbled through his description of his life with his wife.

He told Coy how worried he had become about his training with the government and armed service. He knew he was trained as a killer. In fact, he felt that he possibly was the best trained killer in the United States Government. With that, he had in the back of his mind that nothing is built, trained, sculpted, and developed without ever having a chance of being utilized. While he was telling Coy, he became more and more agitated and boisterous like a fully loaded gun ready to be used. Although he did not want to even think about being away from his wife and family, the pull to be useful and needed became overwhelming. He hungered to prove his worth.

It happened! Immediately after December 7, 1941, Growler was picked up right at their small apartment door without notice and, literally, pulled right from the arms of his very pregnant wife. With no explanation of where he was going, he was taken away to be part of the war effort. He did not know and really did not want to imagine he might never be able to come back to his love. He lived with strict orders to live secretly and make no contact with any friends or family and, specifically, his wife. They told him if any of the enemies knew of his wife, she would be endangered, and they probably could not protect her or their newborn child. He was, in all reality trained, as certified killer, spy, and property of the government.

Growler told Coy, with both of his eyebrows raised, "I wanted to be the best and I was, and I still can say I was and am one of best ever! I never asked for the will or skills but as long as this was the will and skill, I was bound by duty to God, country, and myself to conform and be the best."

Growler looked up towards the white building and sat in silence.

Nothing was lost from the moment, which subsided. A glimpse of life was what it took to set Growler free when he allowed history and memory to be something not to be forgotten. He sang it out beautifully for the audience of one.

Coy did not ask questions as Growler spilled his history like a broken dam of water needing new and more space. Coy received a glimpse of this man's life, and it was tantalizing. Even though he was a young man on a journey with another, Coy somehow knew when to stop and just listen and absorb.

The fishing had stopped and each of them had already neatly tucked their poles in position by the oars. Coy estimated together they had ten or twelve nice bluegill keepers. Growler pulled up the anchor and carefully rinsed the slimy mud off it before lifting it into the boat. Coy started the motor, and they made their way eastward and back out of the narrow strait entrance into Jordan's Bay. Growler bellowed out over the sound of the motor and spoke for the last time on this day, "Well, here we go east of Eden again."

Coy maneuvered the boat and headed directly back to Dock 1, and as usual the resort was humming with life; kids were swimming off Dock 3 on the anchored raft about twenty feet out into the bay. There was laughing, screaming, and splashing. Coy could see Gary and Jimmy over on Dock 7, wetting a line and trying to catch some fish.

Coy surveyed the entire shoreline of the resort when they were a few hundred yards off shore. He thought it was quite a view, at least what life Coy could reckon. He saw a car entering the resort and heading behind the cabins, and he could see it was the folks from Cabin 7. They were all jammed in their station wagon and coming back from somewhere.

Now, more than ever, Coy needed to go meet and greet those folks. He wanted to know why anyone would leave the resort on a beautiful Sunday morning.

The boat was docked with ease and precision. They sat in the boat at the dock, and Coy looked at Growler and found the mysterious Growler was present again but now with a mysterious answered glimpse.

Growler jumped out of the boat first and stood on the dock, looking over the lake with a knowing stare. He caught a glimpse of Coy and immediately turned around and grabbed the five-gallon pail on the end of the dock and brought it back to the boat. Coy was still sitting down on the back seat of the boat and emptied the fish basket. Even though he had counted the fish already by habit he counted a baker's dozen of bluegills from the basket and put them in the pail and finished up the task. He stepped out of the boat. Growler was standing right on the edge of the water next to the dock, washing his hands. They made eye contact as Coy stepped off the dock and headed in the direction of the fish house, and Growler followed. Coy could not help thinking that despite appearances, Growler could not be judged a pessimist, as his face was shaped with a natural smile look, even if it was not a smile. For Coy to judge anything different would be essentially a total loss of faith in the human condition. With everything Coy had heard and learned this morning, Growler might have been born without any judgment to lose.

They stepped into the fish house and, with efficiency and without a spoken word, cleaned the fish. This time Growler did the final cleaning by the small sink and put the fish in a smaller pail and washed them again. Without acknowledgment, Growler opened the fish house door and started his trek back to Little Mora. Coy cleaned up the fish house, grabbed the small bar of soap next to the sink, and washed his hands. He splashed water on his face until he felt refreshed as he tried to figure out what time of the day it had become. Before he finished his thoughts, the bells started ringing out with purpose.

At noon on Sundays, the bells from the white building on the hill made their final advent. Coy heard the bells before but this time when he heard the sound, his ears were ringing and his heart was feeling. Seven rings of the bells to the tune of "Jesus loves me this I know." Coy sang along.

CHAPTER 28

Over to Cabin 7

Coy decided it was time to stop by and get in the tree swing and collect his thoughts. He did know what his mind was seeking. He could not help thinking that what had just happened in his life was far-reaching and overwhelming. No one had ever dumped that much information upon him in one sitting. He thought about what it must be like being old. He pondered what he might become and what direction his life would take. Most troubling of all was that he wished he would have a known skill like Growler had in his youth, and he hoped it wasn't about killing. He took off his shoes, freed his feet, and leaned back in the swing to stretch and relax. Even though his body began to relax, his mind was stirring just like the fish in Jordan's Bay, stirring up the mud and creating the cloudiness in the water.

He swung around and noticed the back of the station wagon he had seen coming into the resort. It was parked behind Cabin 7. He was pleased with himself as he had it right that it was the Cabin 7 folks. Well, time was a moving, and it was time to stroll on over and check them out.

He sprang out of the swing with his mental energy back and started making his way over to Cabin 7. He began to worry, as he needed to have a reason to go over there. He needed some reason to infringe upon their time and space just in case El was not there. He came up with the idea of checking the Franklin stove and telling them he was coming over to make sure everything was working okay.

He wandered between Cabins 6 and 7 and could see a few folks sitting around the wooden tables in front of the cabins. He was walking between the cabins and looked intently around to see if he could spot Emmanuel. He didn't see him, but the older gentleman sitting on the far end of the table in front of Cabin 7 spotted Coy.

"Hi, son, how are you doing this morning?" The nice older gentlemen spoke up in a welcoming tone.

"I am doing fine. Ah, ah, I came over to check something out in the cabin. Would it be okay for me to check it out?" Coy stumbled in response, but his preparation worked, and his asking was successful.

"Of course, young man. The ladies and Emmanuel are in the cabin. Go ahead and go right in," the nice gentlemen replied.

"Thank you," Coy replied.

Coy looked at the man and felt a graceful presence. He walked in front of the table and made his way to the door of Cabin 7.

The inner wood door was open, but the screen door was closed. Coy knocked three times at the same time he opened the door, made a few steps in the cabin and announced, "Resort business, I am here to take a look at a few things." He walked past the front couch and turned the corner to the kitchen area and came upon an older woman preparing to make some coffee at the small stove. She immediately asked if he would like a cup of coffee. A younger woman was standing behind one of the kitchen chairs, where a young girl of about eight years old was sitting and giggling while her hair was being combed gently with bows in hand.

"Hello, fine ladies. My name is Coy. I am a representative of the resort, here to check on your wood stove over there in the corner. Is everything working fine with the stove?" Coy asked, speaking with a clear and precise tone.

"Why yes, it is working fine, young man," the older woman by the stove responded.

"Well okay then, ah, ah... do you know where Emmanuel might be?" Coy asked.

"He is in the bedroom taking his church clothes off," the young girl answered. While she was answering, Emmanuel stepped from behind the sheet doorway of the back bedroom.

"Hi Coy, what's up?" Emmanuel asked.

"Hi, buddy, just checking if you want to hang out a bit and have some fun." Coy changed his thought process while answering in his resort welcoming committee voice.

"This is my mother, and my grandmother, and sitting here is my sister, Mary." He introduced them while warmly looking at each of them.

"Very nice to meet you all, and sorry about the intrusion. I am happy your stove is working fine. In reality, I just wanted to meet you all. Emmanuel, do you want to throw the Frisbee or play some catch or something?" Coy asked with confidence.

"Ya, that would be fun," Emmanuel replied while looking at Coy.

Coy felt welcomed, and he had a nice feeling about Emmanuel. Emmanuel felt the same way.

"Would that be okay, Mother?" Emmanuel asked.

"Of course, have fun. But before you two run off, do you want a sandwich or something to eat? You must be hungry as it's been few hours since breakfast before we went to church service," his mother said.

"I am a little hungry. How about you, Coy?" He looked at Coy while asking.

Coy realized he was hungry also, but did not want to be a bother, but replied, "Ya, ya, I am hungry."

"Great, Mother, help me make these fine young gentlemen a couple sandwiches," she said, while looking at the older woman by the stove.

This was the first time Coy would eat anything inside one of the cabins with any of the resort guests. He was invited, and he liked Emmanuel.

They hurriedly ate up the delicious ham and cheese on toasted rye bread sandwiches with German potato salad and a glass of cold milk. It was Coy's first solid lunch since he had been at the resort, and it was delicious.

They finished up, and Emmanuel asked his mother if they could be excused. His mother responded. "Of course, go and have some fun, boys."

They walked out of the cabin. Coy was impressed and thought how nice a family Emmanuel was a part of and he, for a moment, missed his mom and dad and, especially, his sister Debbie.

They walked in front of the cabin, and Emmanuel introduced Coy to his grandfather and his younger brother Joseph, who were playing a game of cribbage. The background of Emmanuel's life became larger. Emmanuel asked Coy to show him around the resort.

CHAPTER 29

The Walk

"Remember to call me El," was the first thing he said as the two friends went out of earshot from the cabin.

"Oh yes, okay, for sure," Coy responded.

"Show me around, Coy. Tell me a story, perhaps your story," El requested.

"Don't you just want to throw the football or a Frisbee? How about we go and swing from that big tree into the water by Dock 2?" Coy responded.

"Ya, maybe, but show me around first. Let's take a walk, and you can be my personal host," El continued.

"Well, okay. I do not know all the answers, but to start this out right, let's head over to the far west end of the resort by the campers." Coy pointed westward as he spoke.

They turned around and walked behind the cabins toward the west end of the resort. Here they were, a couple of people without a real worry in the world.

"I have never met an Emmanuel before, oh, I mean El. Hey, where are you from?" Coy asked, while leading a couple of steps ahead of El.

"Our family is from Chicago. Both my mother and father lived in a neighborhood very close and northwest of Midway Airport. My father works in accounting for a firm near the airport, and my mother is well-educated and decided to be a homemaker. She watches other kids during the daytime and works at the corner Rexall drugstore one night a week and Sunday evenings. We live northwest of Chicago and a bit out of the black neighborhood." El continued to talk as they approached the woods on the far west side of the resort.

"What do you mean black neighborhood?" Coy asked.

"You know, where almost all the people are black," El responded.

"What do you mean black?" Coy continued.

"Don't you see that we are Negroes? I suppose you live in a white neighborhood?" El asked.

"No, no not really, we live in a Catholic neighborhood, 'cause Sacred Heart Catholic church is right down the street from us," Coy responded.

"Are you a Catholic?" El asked.

"No, but most of my friends are. We are Lutherans, and my Great-aunt Edna reminds my dad about that whenever we are at family picnics. She will always bring it up and say, 'You know, young man, we are Missouri Synod and not Wisconsin Synod believing Lutherans.' I really do not know what that all means, and you know what, El? I really do not care," Coy added. "What are you guys?"

"Well, we are believers in our Savior Jesus Christ, and we go to a Baptist church where the services are loud and fun. But we go to different places when we go on vacation. I don't think we are too picky about all that either," El said, while now walking right next to Coy and putting his arm around him.

"What's a Baptist, anyway?" Coy asked.

"I don't really know the whole story. I think, we think we seem to get it more than the Catholics and the Lutherans, I guess, or should I say the Missouri Synod folks." El chuckled as he said it and went on. "But that probably isn't true and not nice to say."

"Probably so." Coy finished up the conversation even though he had no idea why he answered that way. "Well, here we are. The land goes a hundred or so yards farther in those woods up that hill. This also is as far as the people who cleared this land for the resort wanted to go. If you look straight through the trees, brush, and stuff and up this hill, you can almost see the white building up on top of the hill. It is placed nicely so it overlooks the bay over there." Coy was talking, describing, and pointing all at the same time.

"You mean Hilltop Church, right? I think that is the name of it," El asked.

"Is that what they call that building up there?" Coy answered with a befuddled look, even though he knew the name of the church. He still felt a little embarrassed about how he found out the white building on top of the hill was a church. However, he did think the name was appropriate.

"Before we go on, can I ask you a personal question, Coy?" El continued.

"Well yes, but not too personal, I guess," Coy answered.

"I'm not sure if this is too personal, but here it goes... What is it like being a white person?" El asked with reticence.

Coy turned and looked El up and down from head to toe, looked him in the eyes and carefully examined his new friend.

"I suppose the same feeling you must have, you know... a darker white person," Coy answered with a little giggle.

"Wow, I have never thought about it that way. You do know we are different, and I am black, right, Coy?" El asked.

"Of course, I noticed you have darker skin than me, but God tells us not to judge others and especially not to judge by outward appearances. That was something my confirmation class leader told us this spring, and my mother is constantly telling me that, too. I think it all makes a bunch of sense. I do not want anyone to judge me. Do you?" Coy asked, as he looked El in the eyes.

"Well, no. But we do, don't we?" El said.

"I guess, but not unless we want to, and I don't want to," Coy said, while looking away.

"You know, Coy, I like you. I don't want to see you as a white person either or judge you differently because of it. We had no choice on what shade of color our skin is anyway. My mother once told me someone asked her why she was black, and she answered because she drank too much coffee." El chuckled again as he responded.

"You know, El, I like you. My mother once told me she was asked once why her skin was so fair and white, and she answered she had no choice and if she had she would be much darker. And with that we can think of ourselves as brothers from different mothers!" Coy rolled along and chuckled with El.

"Anyway, this lake is called Lake Esquagamah, and we are actually in the township of Palisade, Minnesota. The Indians who lived here a long time ago named the lake such because it was the last lake. Not sure what that all means, but it is the story I was told about how the lake got its name. It is fed by a river and a small spring over there on northwestern shore line of that bay right over there, which is called Jordan's Bay." Coy spoke with authority and continued.

"The cabin my grandpa lives in and where I am staying right now for a couple more weeks is called Little Mora. It was the first cabin built right after World War II around 1949. It must have been pretty rough going back then. Just think of all the trees they had to clear out of this spot. Then all the other cabins were built, one after the other, as more people started coming up and fishing here. Cabin 7 the one your family is in is the newest and was finished in the mid-sixties. This cleared out area here is for the campers and tents," Coy continued as he pointed and described.

"The old house over there is Martha's. Some people call her Goldie. No one understands the nickname as she has dark curly brown hair. Her family was the original owners of this land, and she is the last person alive from her family. She's really busy and tries really hard towards resort, but has to work at the turkey factory in Aitkin during the days so we don't see her much. She is a bit rough around the edges and can barely speak English, more half-German and half-English and maybe a little Indian language or something.

It's fun listening to her," Coy said as he ended the explanation.

"What else?" El asked.

"What else, what?" Coy asked.

"What else makes this place so special?" El asked.

By now the two young men were walking while talking and enjoying each other's company so much they had already made their way behind the big barn area to the southwest corner of the clearing.

"I don't know much, El. My family just somehow was here, I guess. How about your family?" Coy asked.

"Well, we found out about this area from our Uncle Ed, who found out about this place from his boss at the Chrysler plant in Belvidere. He told Ed the fishing was great, and Ed told us. He is with us now. I think you met him," El went on. "I am sorry I asked you how it was being a white person, because I do not like it when I get that question about me… well you know, being black and all."

"No problem, man, no problem. This is the barn where the lawn mower, the tractor, and a whole bunch of junk that helps keep this resort going are kept. That is the gravel road." Coy pointed as he laughed, realizing how silly that comment was. "Hey, where did you guys go this morning? I saw you all coming back in the resort in your station wagon."

"We went to church, you know, Hilltop up there. The pastor is a pretty young man, but, man, for a white guy he can preach. Mother really liked his message today on 1 Samuel, chapter 16, and so did I. You know, humans look at outward appearances, but God looks at the heart," El continued.

"I totally agree," Coy added.

"It was fun," El went on, as he looked across the road at the purple flowers intermingled in the grass in the ditch.

"Wow, I never heard anyone describe church as fun," Coy said.

El turned to Coy and looked him in the eyes as he said, "I suppose it depends on how you define fun. So, let me ask you a question, Coy. What is your definition of the opposite of fun?"

Coy was taken aback a bit and said, "I never thought about it that way. But let me think…" He hesitated. "I guess boredom or misery or some other kind of words I cannot think of."

"Do you go to worship or just go to church, Coy?" El asked.

"Well, I do not know how to answer. We go to church when we are supposed to or can. Especially now, since I am finishing up my confirmation class. Mom and Dad want to make sure I get confirmed. Sometimes on the way home from church, Dad will say, 'Well we got that done now.'" Coy was looking down as he finished his thoughts.

"What are you confirming, Coy?" El asked.

The boys sat down on the ditch embankment and as they did, Coy began, "Well, since I am almost confirmed, I should know that question. Let me think..." He vacillated and then went on. "I am supposed to be confirming that I now am old enough and should know what it is all about. No wait! I am confirming I am now able to figure it all out because of my age and maturity. No wait! I am confirming um, um..." He stopped, and his mind kept stirring around thoughts.

El did not say a thing and let Coy stew on it for a while.

"Okay, I got it. I am confirming my baptism into the belief or something," Coy finished.

"Not bad, Coy. Do you believe?" El asked.

"Ya, of course," Coy answered.

"So why do you go to church then?" El asked.

"Because Mom and Dad go, and they want my sister and me to also, I guess," Coy answered.

"Going to church is not an obligation or a game, Coy. It is where we worship God and our Savior with praise and have enjoyment and fun!"

El knew it was time to let the subject go. He stood up and as he did, Coy did as well. Both knew they had not really finished or decided on anything. Nonetheless, they looked at each other and both knew they were looking at a kindred spirit, even though they were so different in backgrounds and looks.

"Hey, do you want to throw the football around?" Coy asked.

"Yes, that would be fun," El answered.

They laughed heartily together as they both went into action at the exact same time.

CHAPTER 30

Back to Growler's World

A few days later, Coy was back on his regularly scheduled detective work.

He was back in Little Mora alone again, wanting to read more from Growler's book. Coy figured out the daily routines of Grandpa and Growler and knew the times he would have the opportunity to do his detective work all alone in Little Mora. As usual, he thought it best and fun to be serendipitous and let the book open to whatever God meant him to learn. This day it landed at...

> Doubt takes us away, and faith brings us back. My observation concludes we live with habits in a world filled with simpletons. This life seems to be filled with people who value what is worthless and disdain what is priceless. People wink at perversity and wince at morality. Men and women embrace what is foolish and reject true wisdom. I live with the concern we are designed naturally to be all ignorant with diversity.

One Lifetime Is Not Enough!

Sometimes I feel like a man in a story looking in a mirror, seeing no reflection, or sometimes a man in a dream who stretches out a hand to visible objects and gets no sensation of touch. Am I one of the ignorant?

Coy knew he had a small window of time this day, and the real reason he was in the cabin was to tidy it up a bit. However, Coy's curiosity about Growler was piqued a few times each day, and especially during the alone time during chore time. One of the day's chores was to straighten up the cabin, open the two small windows and air it out. The stench of the fry pan cooking and smallness and confined living area always left a lovely familiar smell. He knew he had at least a few minutes to sneak a peek. Growler was on the lawnmower and Grandpa was working on a five-and-a-half Mercury motor out by the shed next to the garage on the other side of the resort.

He looked around and didn't detect anything and tried to continue reading, but his thoughts wandered. He remembered sitting out by the fire the night before with Growler, Grandpa, and a few resort patrons. Coy reasoned, while watching and listening, that most grownups and, for that matter, all people lived in a state of fakery or phoniness. What they said and so many of their actions were for impression and hope of some kind. Often, in one-on-one conversations, a small confession would go Coy's direction in the old statement of, "What you see and hear, Coy, is really not who I really am..." Coy was so confounded by people's overwhelming desire to not be who they were to be all the time.

"Why do people not want to be who they are?" Coy murmured, as he sorted through the small, one-inch pile of beat-up pages and notes in the book Growler had hidden not so discreetly by his bed on the lampstand shelf.

Somewhere in the pile of notes and the small book in his hand was a whole pile of life that Growler noted and wanted to make sure he wrote down and conveyed a reality. Coy had more than an ordinary need to see, feel, and know. He had a mission of awakening rattling his essence of being that could not be left alone.

Coy always read from Growler's book thinking it could be one of the last times he would be able to read from it every chance he had. He also knew time was always of the essence. He never knew if Growler would hide the book better or just keep it with him. Coy leafed through the pages quickly, hoping for a jewel, hoping for the last coin needing to be found. He was startled when he heard a shuffle and a voice or something outside, and he feared someone would walk in the cabin. If not Growler, just someone looking for Grandpa or something. So, the mission, as usual, was under duress.

He then stopped at a page. The title on the top of the page said: *How to be Happy.*

CHAPTER 31

How to Be Happy

The writing was broken and a bit haphazard, like it had been written at different times and under the cloud of anxiety. Coy wondered what was happening in the world right at the moment Growler decided to write down these thoughts.

> Ps19:8 says, "The statutes of the LORD are right, rejoicing the heart."

Coy wanted to find a Bible right away to see if this was from the Bible, and why in the world this would be written here.

"*The word of GOD converts—then it makes me wise—OH WHY, WHY?*" was written very sloppily and obviously under duress of some sort. *Maybe*, as Coy thought, *under hidden cover somewhere in the world*, as his heart was filled with romantic promising thoughts.

"*You only go around once, so go for the gusto kid... fool me once, shame on you, fool me twice shame on me.*" Then it ended with one statement:

"Please cause my heart to rejoice!"

Coy stopped right there, carefully put the pages back in place, stuffed the notes back exactly as he had found them, and put the book faithfully back on the lampstand shelf where it had been before he entered its world. He then finished the cabin chores by dumping the water bucket under the sink out the door. He left the outside wood door open, but shut the screen door and walked out into the outside world and the other Growler world.

Coy was beginning to see a man's life could be described by words and thoughts. Even so, that did not make it any easier.

CHAPTER 32

So, How Many Fish Do You Think Are in the Lake?

———◉———

Coy's senses were on high alert as he stepped out the door of Little Mora. His ears perked up as he heard the music from the radio sitting in the window sill, which was positioned cleverly as it could be heard clearly from within the cabin, and the immediate area around the cabin, including the north side of the cabin where the two makeshift stands were for outboard motors to be mounted for repairs.

"That was George Hamilton IV's big hit in 1967, 'Break My Mind,' and up next is Lefty Frizzell with, 'If You Got the Money,'" the soft-spoken words from the radio DJ told his radio audience, including Coy.

Coy had no clue what the song was about. However, it did have a catchy tune and he began to sing along softly. "Break my mind, break my mind oh Lord... 'cause if you leave, you're going to leave a babbling fool behind.... Break my mind..."

Coy's thoughts were in a literal mind-breaking mode, distracted from the mystery of Growler, and had no clue of the love song's undertone. He also jumped for no reason from the familiar sound of the slamming screen door. He heard the lawnmower off in the distance. He knew it was now time for a little Coy time. He began walking slowly to the lake as if there was a pull toward the refreshment. He decided to make his way to Dock 1, where he wanted to just sit on the end of the dock to think and relax. He was happy to find the dock vacant of any people. The Little Mora boat was tied up on the east side of the dock as usual. Once down by the lake, he looked to the west to see what was going on with the resort. All the other docks had people and commotion to overcome, like small kids fishing for sunfish or sunbathing middle-aged women. However, something really caught his eye and attention as he looked over at the docks. He noticed, on the dock in front of Cabin 2 west of Grandpa's dock, the young beauty he had played Scrabble with sitting alone on the end of the dock and dangling her feet in and out of the water. She appeared to be mesmerized and deep in thought.

Coy normally would bypass the prospect to do a meet and greet after his revelatory Growler investigation. He would rather go off and be alone for a period to decompress and collect his thoughts. But she was cute, and he felt the need to just be Coy, and he was interested.

He took a detour and walked over to Dock 2 and stepped carefully onto the dock from the shoreline, covertly, to not be detected. She did not look up and appeared to not notice. He walked softly, bent over, took off his shoes, and sat next to her within a few feet and started dangling his toes in the water. It was refreshing, yet he had preoccupations to overcome and was distracted.

He looked down in the water and could see sunfish and perch swimming around and, as usual, he always wondered if Moby Dick was down there in the depths of the water. He had a slight fear of water, something he inherited from his dear mother. He was mesmerized by watching the fish, and the weather was a perfect mid-seventies temperature. However, there was a very noticeable nice smell coming from the young lady sitting next to him entering his space, He kept looking at his feet as they touched the surface of the water, and he moved the water around with his feet. He noticed the dark black hair growing out from the top of his big toes. His thoughts were clustered and kept coming back with wonder, thinking about what was happening to his body as hair was growing out of new places. In addition, he was noticing a few times a day he had trouble talking and, occasionally, a funny sound would come out when speaking. People kept saying, "Coy's voice is a-changing..."

Everything was changing, like this newfound funny feeling while sitting next to a girl. He had no idea what was happening. Even though her name was forever etched in his soul, he mumbled, "Oh God, what is her name again? My God, I should remember and know." He softly mumbled, hoping she would not hear.

"My name is, well... let me make you guess. Remember we played Scrabble together a few days ago. I do not blame you for not knowing, you were surrounded by all of us, and it must have been weird being the only boy," she softly and sweetly responded.

"Hi, ah, ah, thank you, thank you. Do you remember my name?" he asked with some kind of newfound meekness.

"Of course," she replied. "My mom and aunties affectionately call you 'the cute boy you should get to know better.'" She spoke with a soft, sweet intelligence.

For some reason, Coy felt a warmth that permeated everything. Even the newfound black hair on the top side of his big toes rose to attention. He realized he was in an absolutely new world. He remembered his grandpa and uncles when they would say to him, "Do not be afraid to jump into the deep end occasionally, Coy." Somehow, some way, he did not even have to jump into the deep end, he landed there from outer space and right on the edge of this dock with a cute girl who knew his thoughts, language, feelings, and name.

"Say the truth you're carrying in your heart like a hidden treasure," she recited toward Coy, hoping he might mutter an intelligent response.

Coy sat in silence and listened to her sweet voice. He did think of himself as a bright young man. He always did very well at school. He read more and hungered for knowledge much more than his friends, but he was not a real reader. He liked books, but there just was not a lot of open reading and discussion at home with his mother and father. His mother read novels for pleasure, but it was not the type of reading a mother discussed with her son. The only reading he saw his father do was motorcycle magazines or magazines on machining. Being in confirmation classes this past spring, he was forced to read the Bible but other times when he did pick up the Bible, it was mostly to just move it out of the way.

This young lady he was sitting next to, on a beat-up old wood dock in northern Minnesota, was an obvious reader and to Coy, a real intellect. He instinctively knew he would have to be careful not to expose himself as just another nincompoop or, worse yet, just another Pojken. It was somewhat of a dilemma for Coy, as women in his immediate family were not supposed to be intellects. They were the cooks, washers, doers, and for looking at. This young lady must be that enigma Grandpa thought all women had the potential to be. Just a few months earlier, the leader of his confirmation class, a newly married man of around thirty, was explaining the intellectual equality of men and women in society and saying that men had better figure it out. That subject matter just hit Coy across the bow and began a pounding dance surfacing on his forehead.

Funny how memories jumped into moments of time. A commercial, a conversation, a school lecture, or a song on the radio seemed to spark an interest or thought many days or years later, sticking like the smell of fish guts on your hands after cleaning fish for an hour. The smell of the fish did not go away easily. Coy looked down at his hands and noticed they were a little dirty and, probably, smelled a bit from his earlier chores. So, he leaned down and did a quick wash in the cool lake water and wiped his hands dry on his shirt. He was trying desperately to freshen up without her noticing.

She spoke up to break the silence. "Do you need a towel or something?"

Coy mumbled back a response with a shy look. "Oh no, I will be okay, um, um, thanks."

"Do you read much, Coy?" She spoke inquisitively with hope and anticipation. From outward appearance the answer was obvious, but she had hope. She now remembered from her confirmation class and began to recite silently while looking away and out toward the lake, 1 Samuel 16:7: "But the LORD said to Samuel, Look not on his countenance, or on the height of his stature: because I have refused him: for the LORD seethe not as man seethe; for man looketh on the outward appearance, but the LORD looketh on the heart." or something like that, as she hoped a David-type character was sitting next to her.

Tess was a very bright young lady. She had loving, caring parental support from one parent who loved with charity, working and living with anticipation of an everlasting life and not just a now life. Together, they would read Shakespeare, Chaucer, Melville, Joyce, and a litany of other greats, and they would spend hours discussing them. A mother-daughter bonding time was invaluable and forever lasting.

"The evil man does lives after them. The good is often interred with their bones." She spoke up confidently again, looking outward, but with the hope of audience participation. Tess really was not hoping to show supremacy, and that was the last thing on earth or heaven she wanted. She was hoping desperately for a compadre, other than her mother, with whom she could have an intelligent conversation. All her cousins and friends were just not fun to talk with, and their mundane games, chores, and goofing around girlie games a typical thirteen-year-old would enjoy. She desired something more and something different.

Coy did not hear the words clearly because he was distracted by her nice smell and other things. He was bright enough to say, "Ah, Bach, or... um, one of those really smart folks..." And as he finished, he realized how stupid it must have sounded.

After that initial stumble, he continued with, "Please say that again, that was pretty cool." Coy spoke up with a bit more command.

Even though he knew he was obviously outmatched here, he surely was not going to let on, especially because she was a girl. Showing weakness early on could get you an early warm cookie, but it could eat you up and bury you in the long run when it came to intellectual discussion. Coy had no idea why, when, or even how he knew this concept. It had to have been latently put in him from the start of life.

"Wait." Coy stopped the young intelligent beauty from continuing with her testing diatribe. Just his apparent recognition of the situation and moment took the young lady aback and impressed her.

"Okay..." she slowly and clearly said with a bit less authority. "What or how or when or whatever would you like to talk about, Coy?" she said with a little trepidation.

"Well, to start with..." He stopped as if to think through carefully his next thoughts, when actually he stopped just because it seemed like the right thing to do. "I absolutely know your name is Tess. How many fish do you think are in this lake?" He spoke in a warmer clear voice, making sure to avoid mishap or any harm in the presence.

She laughed. Then stopped in amazement. She really was wondering if he was that smart, or just not smart enough to move on to her level, or whether he was just trying to stall.

Every scenario had possibility, and without hesitation, from deep in her soul she found wonderment in the conversation with this young man, in her space, sitting next to her. Perhaps, she thought it might be best to find out a few things about him. Being so very well taught from the females in her life, she knew how, like a fine sculptor, to smooth the rough edges away to see and feel the real.

"Thank you so much for remembering my name. However, I believe that question would be impossible to answer, Coy," she responded.

"Perhaps, but wondering if evil lives after death seems like a pretty tough question, also," he responded with confidence.

The hairs on the back of her neck awakened as if something or someone from another life blew cold and hot air at her at the same time. She could not believe it; he heard her, and he had diverted the conversation and responded with an unanswerable response.

"This game is afoot!" She put her imaginary Sherlock Holmes hat on and spoke in the best English accent she could muster. We can enjoy playing games when we adhere strictly to the rules. But she wondered deeply if she or he knew the game they were really in.

"Sure is warm today. It is a nice summer day, don't you think?" Coy continued.

Somewhere from the past or, perhaps, it was just a built-in concealed talent, he knew how to control a conversation and how to divert its destiny. He also would be a complete fool if he underestimated this young lady sitting next to him on the dock as they dangled their feet in the cool water below just enough to touch their toes in the water and, once in a while, dunking the whole foot in for refreshment.

"Ya... Ya, I mean yes, yes, it surely is a nice and warm summer day," she responded.

"So, how many fish do you really think are in this lake?" Coy continued with a question he knew was impossible to answer. He began to feel a sense of niceness somewhere down deep. He did not know where it was coming from or how deep of a vault it came from. He had no idea how it got in him, but every time she spoke with her soft, high, and sweet voice, he had an affection that would jumble up his thought process. The words she spoke became just words with little meaning, and he realized he needed to pay much more attention. The whole scene and conversation were a treasure to Coy, and he realized it during each moment.

"I have no idea how to answer that question and, in fact, I believe the question is unanswerable." She spoke with an authoritative and teacher-like quality. She was not ready to sidestep the challenge.

"You are most likely correct with that answer. Madam, would you like to have some crumpets now?" Coy could barely finish saying 'crumpets' without a laugh and as some people close to him would say, that devilish inherited smirky look.

However, he did not want to be that person with her. He wanted to be real and really find out who she was. This was a new moment and a feeling he had never felt before with a girl. He wanted to see if he could get to know her at a different level. Who was she really? His mind was thinking and spinning while trying to be a little less diffident. Without knowing, he was playing something like a scene in life that was playing out before him like vignettes from a mystery novel, and he had no idea if he was an author, reader, or audience. He just liked being part of it all.

"You do not have to answer that question, and I am sorry I started that course of action, but let's play a little game and go back and forth and see who can come up with the most unanswerable question or questions. Mine will be the fish question, and now it is your turn, Tess." He called her by name for the first time and looked her right in the eyes. To him they were a color and hue that could not be described, other than they were deep and beautiful and forever.

It was starting to come to him that every other girl who would cross his path for the rest of his life would be compared to the direct look in Tess's eyes as he sat on an old beat-up dock, looking over a very regular lake in Northern Minnesota, while dangling his twelve-year-old feet into cool water along with hers.

"Okay, smarty pants, let me ask this question of you: Does a mother have to love her kid?" she asked with much less authority and with a deep and cracking voice.

"Well yes, yes, well I think yes," Coy responded with a concerning undertone and without any time to hesitate and think about it. He loved his mother very much and knew his mother loved him and cared for him, and there would be no other palatable answer that could come from his mouth. He remembered his English teacher telling him this past spring to chew on it a bit more before he just spit out the answers in class. This had now become one of his desires to learn, but Coy still struggled with the hesitation.

"I need to ask a follow-up question before we can consider that an unanswerable question. Would that be okay?" He looked over at her but did not look directly at her as he asked the question.

"Well, okay then. What is your follow-up and, maybe, we need some ground rules?" she responded as if to get back in control.

He had not even really looked at her other than at her eyes or even noticed that she was a very stunning young lady of about twelve or thirteen years old. And, for the first tangible moment in his life and at that exact moment, Coy finally adhered to judging by the inward appearance and not the outward appearance in all other relationships with friends and foes in his life. She was so much more than a symbol of the opposite sex; she was his perspective.

A moment of blessing transcending time can become the moment of time when one realizes they are living with deep embedded ideals implanted by God. Coy was starting to understand blessings but surely had no interpretation of a timeless blessing. He was given something this morning, sitting on a dock in northern Minnesota, that would be with him through eternity.

"Okay then..." Coy hesitated because he really had two questions, and he was acutely aware the right question asked was of utmost importance.

"Why the mother? How about the father's love?" he choked out before he had a chance to take it back.

Tess turned and looked right at Coy. "That is an unfair question!" "Why?" Coy responded with little emotion.

"Well, you know, you know, my daddy is no longer here to have the chance to show his love, well, you know..." Tess stuttered out her thoughts with emotional flare.

Coy realized even though the water was only a couple feet deep under his feet, he somehow had jumped into the deep end with no life preserver. He had no idea of what he was doing or even why he was in the conversation.

He did stop and hesitate for a bit though, mostly because he could not think of what to say.

"Well, okay, if your daddy was here, would you know he loved you?" he asked her while staring down at the water.

"Yes, of course!" She did not hesitate even a second.

"How do you know?" he responded.

"I just know." Tess spoke, but as she spoke each word was delivered slowly and with brokenness.

"Can you feel your daddy right now? Do you have an image of your daddy right now in your mind?" Coy gathered himself and actually did the unthinkable and touched the top of her hand right when he finished his question. "And if you feel him here with you right now, do you have faith in how he would love you?"

"Yes," she softly said.

Coy and the young lady did not say another word for two or three minutes. They kicked the water with their feet, and the light breeze cooled them off. It was about 10:30 a.m., and the resort was buzzing, radios were playing from each cabin, doors were slamming, and dragonflies were buzzing and eating mosquitoes. Coy did not like dragonflies at all but the fact that they minimized the horrendous supply of the real Minnesota state bug (mosquitos), he was more than willing to like something he did not really understand or like and go with it.

Tess broke the silence. "He was always happy when he wrote to me and always hugged me, and told me that he loved me. I could just feel it. Everyone always would say I am a female mirror image of my daddy, physically, with my eyes, color of my hair, and personality-wise."

"But you have some of your mom in you. Do you feel the same way about your mom?" Coy continued.

"No, not really. She is always busy and especially since we received the bad news about Daddy. She never smiles and looks at me funny." Tess had a small tear trickling down her cheek from her left eye, and Coy noticed it.

"Hey, how many fish do you really think are in this lake, Madam?" He spoke with his perfect broken English accent.

Tess giggled, and the moment subsided. She spoke with a laughing tone and said, "Nine hundred fifty-three thousand, one hundred, and thirteen," she answered while looking out to the west. "I mean twelve; Jimmy just caught one on Dock 5."

Little did Coy know every man in Tess's life from that moment on would become a juxtaposition of Coy.

CHAPTER 33

Row, Row, Row Your Boat

"Hey, I see the Cabin 2 rowboat over there, and it looks like it has water in it from the rain and waves last night. Would you be willing to help me a bit right now?" Coy pointed between Dock 1 and Dock 2.

"What, what... I mean ya, ya, ah, ah, I mean yes, I will help, something to do..." Tess responded clumsily and somewhat hesitantly as the balloon of silence and the weight of the world burst.

They stood up and, for the first time, Coy looked directly at her and noticed she was about the same height, had perfect gorgeous brunette colored hair, smelled very nice, and, of course, had the most beautifully colored eyes he had ever seen. At his older cousin's wedding a few years back, he said a silent prayer on the way home, praying God would find the right girl for him someday when he was older. He had no idea why that thought even popped into his mind. However, he thought if this was God's first attempt at it, he knew God must be listening. This was definitely more than just a base hit.

He noticed for some reason again that he did not smell very good. His shirt was not tucked in, and he remembered he needed to brush his teeth. A memory of his mother talking with him came upon him. He was realizing just about everything his mother would ask him to do every morning while getting ready for school was coming to fruition sooner and unexpectedly. His mind was flowing with remembrances at this inopportune time of everything Mom had been telling him to do for years.

"Make sure you are paying attention, young man," she would always end with. He swallowed some spit a few times, clumsily tucked in his shirt, and his only resolution to the smell was to forget it and blame it on the fish house if the subject came up.

They both got up, put their shoes on, and walked off the dock in single file with Coy leading. He jumped the last few feet to the shore. He did not know why, but he had to prove he could do it. She noticed and took a little more of a run at it, and outjumped Coy by two feet. He, of course, noticed, but concealed his thoughts so she wouldn't now he looked and noticed her winning feat. Coy was well aware girls and boys at twelve and thirteen could be very close athletically. Coy knew it very clearly, as he had earned a second -place finish in the 600-yard dash in gym class before school was out for the summer. The person who earned the first -place finish was a girl named Lisa. He did not know if he would ever like any girls named Lisa again.

He despised that girl and as he expected, she teased relentlessly that he had lost to a girl, which he now thought of as a "Lisa" quality. Coy was hoping the whole experience would eventually be memorialized as a teaching moment in time. Despite the new world he was entering with unknown feelings towards girls, he still felt something way down deep, where he believed that in every aspect girls and boys were equal in God's eye. However, Coy did not think equality meant being exactly alike. Girls were girls, and boys were boys, and God had reasons for both. He could live with that, and he decided just to live with that, but the wound was still there.

Coy noticed Tess was strong and fit and didn't want to judge her or anybody in any way but being fit did say something. Or, as Grandpa might say, "She is a one of the good ones. You know, a husky one!" Or he might say, "She comes from good crop." Coy knew right then and there, this young lady obviously came from a seriously good crop.

Dock 1 was built to be a bit out of the way, and it took a little effort to pay attention to it. Dock 1 was Grandpa's dock, where his boat was docked on the east side. Often, the boat for Cabin 1 was tied to the dock on the west side. The bay the resort was on was crescent moon-shaped, standing on the end of any of the docks allowed a view of all the ends of each of the seven docks. Docks 2 through 7 had two small fourteen-foot Lund boats attached, and the boats would be pulled ashore and tipped upside down when they were not in use, or when there were no occupants at the cabins. Right now, all the boats were in the water, either in use or attached to their respective docks and associated with the occupants of the cabins. Because there with a few boats owned by the patrons, Dock 1 would also be used for other boats besides Grandpa's.

Coy gathered most of the folks would bring a small outboard motor for their cabin boat, as it was sometimes easier than hauling a boat. However, some of the more serious folks would have a nice boat with a bigger motor of maybe a twenty-five or forty horse size. Grandpa would rent out one of his older outboard motors attached to the side of the Little Mora cabin when needed or for backup.

Others would leave the small boats for the younger kids as row boats and leave the motors off, which worked out great because the bays on both sides were full of beautiful bluegill sunfish and rowing out briefly and anchoring in the lily pads carefully in about four feet of water worked. A couple of people could get their fill of fish in an hour or so.

"Hey, how tall are you, Coy?" she asked him, right after she jumped off the dock to the shore.

"Well, let me see..." Coy begin thinking and mumbling to himself in calculation at the same time he started walking to Dock 1. He slowed his pace and briefly thought about why she would be asking this question. But he decided to be specific and open. "Five feet even, and I weigh 98.9 pounds," he retorted.

"Wow, that is pretty specific, and how do you know your exact weight?" she politely asked.

"Well, I just finished wrestling camp, and we got weighed and measured. My overall goal is to grow to about five feet six and weigh no more than 145, maybe 150 pounds. To me, that is the perfect size for a guy. I would be strong enough to do anything," Coy responded with passion.

Wrestling camp brought back another life lesson to Coy, as he learned at heart and in body he really did not like to fight. The weight and size of a man could not truly be measured.

"That sure is specific. Is that how big your father is, or how did you come up with that information?" she asked while they both sidestepped a rough shore area that had become a sprain-your-ankle hole from erosion.

"Just seems right to me," he responded.

"Well, God might have something to say about it, though, don't you think?" she said.

"Of course, but can't we will some of the stuff He wants for us?" he quietly said, knowing just saying it didn't feel or sound right.

Coy noticed how nice the day was becoming as they walked to Dock 1. It was around 11:00 a.m., seventy degrees with a clear blue sky with a few high clouds. He didn't know why that came to mind. He was always aware, and his mind was always moving and operating in several directions, and it worked for him. Unfortunately, some of the teachers at school were constantly trying to get him to focus on one task at a time. Coy decided to go with his God-given ability to multitask and let it just happen. The habit of thinking at multiple levels and with multiple purposes and tasks at one time was not just a skill, it was who he was becoming. He blew those teachers off and knew it was a terrific quality to possess in someone with a lifelong desire to learn. Fighting something that was so natural was a challenge. Coy wondered why he should fight it.

Coy walked purposely enough steps ahead of her to be leading but with earnestness and with no intention of leading. He always desired to be first in everything. However, he wanted to make sure to be first only by purpose, not by reason.

All of his senses were on high alert and he could make out the music and the song coming from the radio sitting in the front window of Cabin 2. The song was familiar, and he recognized that it was Jim Croce's "Bad, Bad Leroy Brown." Coy knew the song well. He and his friend Tommy back at home would hear it on the radio at Tommy's apartment building's community pool about every thirty minutes while they were there swimming and having fun.

He began to sing the words with a deep undertone, "Bad, Bad, Leroy Brown..." Coy was singing while looking the other way, as he was a little embarrassed by his inability to have any tone. He knew he was tone deaf, but not music dead.

Tess's senses were on high alert also, and she, of course, heard him. It was like they had matching alert antennae.

"Hey, I like that song," she said with conviction.

"What, what, oh I am sorry, I like the song and know it, but didn't realized that I was singing it out loud enough to be heard. My inner voice is as great as Elvis's, but my outer voice needs a bunch of work and, maybe, will never work so good," he said with an embarrassed grin.

She understood instantly and could hear and see Coy's discomfort and with empathy said, "You sound great. Don't be so hard on yourself."

Coy accepted the comment with little analysis and, once again, just for that moment he wanted it to be true.

"Why thank you, my dear. You are very nice. Maybe someday I will not mind being heard," he responded.

He remembered something Grandpa told him the night before at dinner time. "Coy, time is the overseer of all things." He would always remember Grandpa saying that and was praying and hoping to understand. Little did he know, that transitory comment would carry him through so much in life.

"Well, maybe with some help, a little luck, and hard work, I will be able to sing at a minimum okay someday. But for now, only the outer world will have to suffer my inabilities." He laughed while talking with his smirky smile.

Tess laughed. Coy liked this understanding person next to him. It wasn't a penchant because she was a girl who was in shape, cute as the dickens, and smelled great, but because she was pretty neat and understood things.

They started walking down the shoreline where the boat was half in the water and half on shore. Coy already was calculating how they were going to complete the task of getting the water out of the boat and tipping it upside down on shore. It looked to be about a third full of water and heavy. At first inspection, the boat situation looked quite daunting. However, a flashback came to his mind from a week or so before his resort time, while he was at the small library at the corner block of Hubbard Avenue and 42nd Avenue. He read an affirmation quote on the wall— "Whether you think you can, or you think you can't—you're right."

The quote caught Coy's eye while he walked capriciously in and out through the children's book area, looking for something fun to read, as he was at that in-between desire time in life between kid stuff and adult stuff. He had to see who said it, as he thought it must have come from one of those old, really wise folks who came up with everything a lifetime or two from the past. Lo and behold, it was from Henry Ford, which made Coy like Ford trucks, even though his family was a Chevy family. It was just another thing he had to keep to himself. He remembered standing there looking and analyzing the thought from Henry Ford and wondering how much of his life was being developed from his parents' habits, and if they would ever let him create his own habits and desires, like something as simple as a car brand.

The first thing considered was obvious. Coy would never be able to do this boat task alone. He immediately had a good feeling, knowing he had help. He thought, "I think I can," and then realized he should actually be thinking, "I think *we* can." His mind was swimming as he jumped into the lake to get a closer look at the boat to see if he could push it on shore. He wondered if it was possible, he had found his female doppelgänger, thinking the exact thing he was thinking right at that exact same time.

He thought it was highly unlikely, but did not know if he liked that there could be someone just like him living on the earth. Tess surely could not be his doppelganger anyway because she was a girl, but it was nice to have her there to help. The doppelganger idea came up the night before in the fish house with the folks from Cabin 6 when Coy helped clean some fish with them.

He looked at Tess, who was still standing on shore waiting for some instructions and noticed how cool it would be to meet his doppelganger. On the other hand, one life was enough sometimes.

What a weird subject to be thinking about. One of the big advantages of being a kid at a resort was having things to do, mind-clearing activities throughout the day and evenings. Coy knew and felt an individual uniqueness about himself, as his mind would not stop and he just could not turn his thought processes off.

"Hey, Tess, do you think you could guide and slightly lift the front of the boat as I push it out of the water to get as much of the boat on shore as we can together?" Coy asked with a tone of leadership and authority in his voice.

"What, what did you call me?" she immediately responded.

"Tess. That is your name, right?" he responded without looking up.

She pondered and looked right at him as she said with an attentive stare, "I like when you call me by my name."

"I have my ways and like some folks in my life would say, you were on my radar." He looked at her as he answered.

"That is pretty cool," she said with a bit of a crooked look. She could not help but be a little taken aback, and a bit smitten by it all.

Coy realized how careful he had been to expose any history or desire her way but in the moment of teamwork and exertion, it just happened.

"Okay, ready and on three, let's try to move the boat up a way onto shore together. Ready, oh wait a second—isn't it funny that none of us would be here without the water of the lake and, in turn, here we are trying to get rid of the lake water from the boat?" Coy asked with a giggle, just knowing that might have been one of those unanswerable questions she was looking for, but also knowing it sure was not some big important thing right at that moment.

"Okay, one, two, and three..." And as he hit the three count, they struggled. However, working together, they were able to guide the boat about halfway up on the shore, but the boat was still half in the water. Coy right there confirmed to himself that this surely gave her a touch of unexpected toughness from what he could tell. Just a little push and the boat was in a position for them to be able to tip it sideways and dump the water out of it. Coy stepped onto the shore as he looked intently at Tess and gave her a smile. She giggled as if she knew she just showed him a little something.

Coy emptied the boat of all debris, oars, and the anchor and with ease and no verbal instruction, they tipped the boat over and upside down on the shore.

"Well, that should do for now, we will leave it as is. Thank you very much, Madam, for your help," Coy politely said as he touched her right forearm, not really understanding the physical implications that happened with a touch.

"Please come to our resort fish fry and campfire tonight. We are leaving tomorrow afternoon." She spoke his way while looking in his eyes.

"Ah, ah, ya, you what? —I will be there," he responded.

Coy turned and looked across the lake and turned his gaze to the shoreline, and noticed the small boat coming in at Dock 6. "Hey, you know what? I think I will check that out," he said as he pointed at the boat coming in and docking at Dock 6. "Hope to see you later, and have a great day, Tess," he politely said and looked right at her.

As he did, she silently melted inside and held her smile with a stern, upright posture. "Me, too... hope to see you later, friend. Off we go," she said as she moved back as if it was her decision to move on.

They were standing between the dock and the big tree that leaned toward the lake and gave shade to about half of Dock 1 and Dock 2 and had the rope swing attached. Coy was wet from the waist down and decided to walk out onto Dock 1 first to clear his mind and dry off, as the sun had the midafternoon blaze and warmth going on down. He recognized that his time and energy drained his thinking, and reacting and talking to other people had time limits. He also knew that if he continued with this course, his unknown untapped weaknesses would surface. Coy had a built-in clock on when his time was up and when he just had to move on. He always sensed that some people thought it rudeness when it was time to cut it off. He thought it was worth the so-called impoliteness, as controlling a situation was much more valuable than showing any form of vulnerability or weakness. He surely did not want Tess to see that side of him.

Tess was still by the shoreline and looked back in Coy's direction. "Hey, by the way, young gentleman, someday I might let someone else besides my father call me Teresa." Tess spoke loud enough for Coy to hear. He did not smirk this time as he looked her way. He had a welcomed warm look on his face and answered with a nod.

He turned around and walked over to Dock 1. She turned and walked the opposite direction. He stepped on the dock and looked over to Dock 6. The folks were docking their boat and securing it to the dock. He sat down on the end of the dock, and he turned to see if he could still see Tess. She had made her way back to her family's cabin area, where there were several family members on lounge chairs enjoying the late morning sunshine and conversation. Teresa was looking back at him at the same time.

CHAPTER 34

Alone Time

Coy felt it was nice to have a chance to be alone with only his thoughts to wrestle and no games of conversation with anyone. He noticed perspiration coming down his forehead and wondered if it was from the sun or his thoughts of what happened in his life the past thirty minutes. He desperately hoped it was the sun but discerned deep down it might be coming from somewhere else. He never remembered liking someone so quickly and sensed from somewhere deep within the well of boyhood that early manhood was surfacing beyond and out of his control. He really liked Tess or as his soul was telling him, he liked what she represented. Tess was a representative from the girl side that he really enjoyed and got. What she had; he could not explain. He just knew something there was special and appealing.

Without making it look like he was following her, he pretended to look at dock 1 for imperfections and some kind of busy work details that would make it look like he had a purpose for being there, when in reality it was a Coy-induced time out. He knew he needed a time out from being Coy.

He walked slowly off the dock but could not help looking her direction. She was back within the confines of her family and friends and appeared to not really care what he was doing. He decided to make a big jump off the dock to the shoreline as if he were an Olympic long-jump athlete when he really knew that he was not even a grade school long-jump athlete. It bugged him right away that he was acting like a kid and that he was acting out without thinking about what was happening. Something had control of him, and he could not explain it. Another life within his life.

Coy started walking around to the backside of Cabin 2. He tried again to look over to where Tess was, and of course it was right when she was looking back at him. He picked up his pace and dodged behind the cabin and walked the long way around the backside of the cabins to make his way down to Dock 6.

CHAPTER 35

The All-Americans

Growler was on the John Deere riding lawnmower, cutting grass near the ditch embankment at the entrance of the resort. Coy could hear the engine. Grandpa was working on an old Johnson outboard motor under the overhang at Little Mora. The resort and all the pertinent people in Coy's life for the moment were doing what he felt they should be doing. However, Coy had a profound feeling that he was not being significant and needed something to do. It was one of those moments during the day when humans felt they need to be doing something and to keep moving, or moss would grow on their brain or external, physical, not-so-discreet areas. With that in mind, Coy had a lingering feeling that he had something of purpose to achieve. It was a strong enough intuition that might have caused beads of sweat to run down his forehead. But for the moment, there seemed like there was nothing better to do than to clean a few fish for the folks in Cabin 6.

Coy was walking behind the cabins in the direction of Cabin 6 when he heard a loud bang and a noisy rattle coming from the direction of the resort entrance where Growler was mowing the lawn along the ditch line. He looked the direction of Growler and deduced he had apparently hit something solid. The mower engine roared from no resistance and then quit running after an initial loud bang. Coy's plans changed in an instant, and off toward Growler he went. However, his ears were aroused while he changed directions and he heard from the radio in the back window of Cabin 4.

"And when I die…well, then let the time be near…" The radio announcer indicated the song playing was a 1969 hit from Blood, Sweat, and Tears.

"Wow!" Coy sputtered out loud. "What a perfect name for a group." He spoke clearly as he sauntered over to see if he could help Growler out.

Coy, now with more focus, walked to Growler. By the time he reached him, he was off the mower and sitting on the embankment at the resort entrance with a brooding look straight up to the sky above Cabin 6 and in the direction of Jordan's Bay. Coy noticed and thought Growler was sitting really close to where he and El sat and talked about what fun was all about.

Coy knew right away he had to get into the direct contact zone with Growler. Growler was in the mystery thinking other place mode, and he knew it would take patience and careful thinking to be with him. Many times, and, often with Growler, the communication began and ended with a loud silence. The noise of the world around never outweighed the real communication. Coy carefully watched communication processes at the nightly campfires and intently watched Growler to see what was being communicated. Coy would move on to another chore or person, as his mind never could calculate if anything had happened, when in reality much information was expelled. From the snarly look on Growler's face, Coy sensed it might be one of those times.

Coy entered Growler's space and world. He thought about how many card games of gin rummy and kings in the corner they had played together in the last couple of weeks. Somehow in the past couple of weeks while building a relationship, Coy and Growler had developed a strong conversational relationship even when no words were spoken. So, often, after an hour or two of playing cards, the mystery of who Growler was would peak. Coy's motivation to decipher and figure him out became an obsession and not just a desire, and Growler conceded it with Coy and played along. After all, some verbal communication was needed, but Coy enjoyed the challenge. It was fun.

Grandpa would intervene occasionally and had periodically, through seasoned advice and foreknowledge, advised Coy there would be times during the day when Growler's mind and spirit were in another universe or time. Coy thought the whole concept to be a bit foreboding. The answers to the mystery of finding out where Growler was or what he was thinking far outweighed anything else for Coy while the summer days moved along. But as usual, Growler did have moments that were daunting to Coy, as he had never seen pondering from way deep beyond the soul from anyone else in his life.

Coy was alive and well in his world with curiosity and an inquiring young man's mind. He was apparently born with an embedded empathy chip somewhere down deep that was always on the prowl for settlement. This summer it settled down with Growler. However, Coy had a deep feeling that all people were all surface and no substance and in a continuing battle of living another life in a world that was not before them. Growler was different as he wasn't really living in the now world and not really in that other past life or the new future life ahead, sitting on the embankment of this old resort with an ominous stare into a far-off place and time.

Coy desperately did not want to be a surface person and was not a surface person. However, there was a really hard surface to break. Coy desired to be the same person on all occasions. He wanted to live in the present and not live a fake life of always wanting to be someone else or somewhere else. He did not want to be bogus, like the calmness of the world right before a big storm crossed the lake while a complete deluge of rain and wind hit the resort and all the folks tried to find shelter. The scene was like the calmness before a storm, which led scared people in all situations. However, often it was in the calmness where the realness of life happened. So to Coy, Growler might have been an enigma and maybe he needed a little Growler in his life to find out what the Coy life really was and could become.

Coy was now standing in front of Growler and looking him in the face. After looking, he knew Growler was in that other world, in a different life, a life with only oneness. Growler's face held a reddened grimace of hate and fury, like the primitive Native American mask Coy had seen at the Minneapolis Art Museum when his sixth- grade social studies class went on a field trip this past spring. What made the mask so chilling to Coy was not the look, but the reason behind the look.

"What is it, Growler?" Coy spoke with an empathetic bend and calmness. He was attempting to enter into the Growler space and life, sitting next to the silent riding lawn mower at the entrance of this obscure lake resort in northern Minnesota. A resort perhaps only 500 people or less in the entire world even knew existed. Coy understood even though this was a very cool place and time to be at this resort in comparison to everything else in the world, it was nothing more than a very small drop of water in contrast to all the water that had ever come down from Heaven. Coy somehow and from somewhere had a God-given talent of not letting the environment around him seem too big or too small, but it often frustrated him by not letting the environment be bigger than it really was. However, sometimes important moments passed him by without notice, and he later recognized how big a moment he missed. Coy struggled with making things too big. He wanted things to be real all the time. But understanding real often took time, experience, seasoning, and sometimes memory.

Coy was looking directly at Growler, and they were face to face. Growler's stare was blank, and he didn't realize Coy was now in his space and time.

"Hey, hey!" Coy spoke up with a bit more fervor. Growler broke from the space and time he was part of and came back to the present or the future.

"What's up, buddy? What happened to the mower?" Coy inquired. From the position Growler was sitting on the ditch embankment, he lowered his gaze from the sky and could now looked straight ahead and right at Coy. Coy knew right away that even if he had not been there at that exact spot, Growler's look would have passed right through him anyway.

"You okay, pal? Do you need some help here?" Coy asked with the gentlest spirit he could muster.

"No, ah yes!" Growler said with his half-German, half-Northern Minnesota Norwegian English accent, so different from the perfect English diction Coy would hear him speak out on Jordan's Bay. Coy loved the tone and wanted dearly to know how a man could have come to the point of not really having a voice other than a mixed batch of cookie dough that tasted better as dough than baked cookies for a speaking voice. Although Coy was pretty happy, as this was the first time Growler spoke to him without being out on the water.

Coy expected a nod or a wink and was not expecting a verbal response; he was taken aback when he heard Growler speak because they were not out on the lake in a boat. This was the first time Growler had spoken to Coy on shore.

"How can I help you, sir?" Coy said with a formal and concerning presence.

"Oh, oh, I am okay, my son, I am back... the belt or something came off, and we need to get the machine over to the tool shed and get it fixed up. Give me a hand, and let's push it over there." Growler spoke now with a much more educated tone. The change from the so-called uneducated to a formal vocal presence only added to the mystery. Coy noticed how careful Growler was with his diction.

Coy looked in the direction of the fish house and the tool shed, south of the fish house, and did a quick estimate of the effort it was going to take. He thought it had the possibility of being a bit of a hassle. However, he also thought working together with Growler would be well worth the effort and reward. Coy grasped Growler's right forearm and shirt sleeve and helped the older man get to his feet. Once Growler got to his feet, he stepped back, raised his left eyebrow, looked down now at Coy, and silently acknowledged the thought and effort this young man was giving. Growler had so often lived a solitary life and having a little help from another life was welcome.

The air was thick while the weather for the day was getting warmer. There was a brief awkward silence; it was as if both of them realized they were perspiring even though they had not really done much physical effort. Coy took Growler's lead, and they got behind the mower. The drive belt had popped off when Growler hit a solid surface or an exposed rock on the ditch embankment at an awkward angle. Pushing the machine together was fairly easy without the motor resistance. The summer warmth was coming in as usual this morning, and they definitely were sweating while pushing the machine in the direction of the shed. Nevertheless, the unique experience of people working together, sweating together, breathing hard together, and moving forward with and for a common cause and purpose became a natural bonding experience.

"Growler, may I ask you a question, sir?" Coy spoke up from the back side of the machine while he pushed.

Growler was guiding the steering wheel and pushing from the right side. They were in close proximity but not in each other's personal space. Coy also had a problem with personal space intrusion as Growler surely did.

"Yes, you may," Growler responded. His response was with a perfect tone, and with educated, impeccable English accent. Coy noticed right away again that when Growler let his guard down just a bit, he would come across as a very well-read and educated man.

The moment of time and the occasion might have thrown Coy off his game as he had pondered this thought and obvious observation of Growler since the first time he met him at the very instant he was dropped off at the resort. Coy could not get it out of his head why this man, who obviously was very smart and with some kind of vast and interesting past, would want to be a Growler and identified as a stupid or distant dummy relative, with no apparent discernible life or past interest to anyone.

"Is Growler your real name?" Coy asked with a thoughtful look and feel.

"No, no it is not, why do you ask?" Growler mumbled in his Growler mixed speech of half-German and half-Northern Minnesota Norwegian.

"Just wondering, I guess..." was all Coy could muster up in response.

They were at the half-opened overhead entrance door to the tool shed. Growler let go of the wheel and stepped back then started towards the shed to look for some tools. Coy stopped pushing and followed him into the worn-down old barn-like building, which measured around twenty-four feet wide by forty feet long. The building was filled to the roof with old outboard motor parts, yard tools, old life preservers, decrepit lawnmowers, beat-up old lawn chairs, and a bunch of junk. The overriding impression was the smell of gas that had aged with a slight tinge of turpentine smell, dirt, and old age. But to a twelve-year-old, the shed was a field day of exposure to a life past.

They walked almost side by side with Growler a small step ahead. They reached the front overhead sliding wood door and, together, they fully pushed open the door.

While working together in opening the door, Coy said, "Why, Growler?"

"It is my mononymous designation of distinction, young man," he answered with clear English.

Coy did not know what that meant. He was starting to think Growler might not even know his own name.

"My name is Coy, and it is very nice to meet you, Growler, or older young man, or whatever your real name may be," Coy responded with a knowing smile.

Growler growled and muffled a chuckle then laughed out loud.

"Back behind the fish house there are a couple of wood blocks. Please go get them, so we can block up the side of the mower and take a look at the belt situation." Growler spoke with clear English.

"No problem." Coy was thankful for the nice asking process and responded as he walked out the side door of the shed and to the fish house located just twenty-five or thirty feet north of the shed.

Coy grabbed a couple of the pieces of wood that were about twelve inches by twelve inches. He was able to carry them, one in each hand and under his arms. They were heavy, but he was not going to let on that there was any difficulty with completing the task before him. When he stood up with the wood, he noticed a few folks walking toward the fish house with a couple baskets of fish, and pans for their cleaned morning catch. Coy nodded their way, smiled and moved on back to the front of the shed. He realized he had just done a "Growler." Coy made his way to the lawnmower, and Growler was still in the shed, looking carefully for something. Coy dropped the blocks by the mower and went back to the shed.

"Hey, what you are looking for?" Coy inquired.

"Looking to see if there are any spare belts just in case the belt is broken or spliced," Growler responded and a few seconds later spoke out in space without taking his eyes off his search, looking up at the walls and shelves. "See if you can locate anything that looks like a belt."

"It's really messy in here. We'll have to dig around a bit. It sure looks like shelves of different sizes as well as the bench were built just where they were needed at any given time including the bench. Things seem to be left in place and set down right where it was convenient or a chore was completed," Coy said with an inquisitive lower tone while looking around.

"You are most likely correct son. I mean to say Coy, if that is your real name," Growler responded.

"Thank you," Coy said with a caring undertone.

Coy was taken aback, as it was the first time Growler actually spoke Coy's name out loud. He was befuddled and thought back to the many hours sitting in the boat alone with Growler, or at the fire in the evenings with the crowd, or the hours out and in the boat, or playing card games together, or all the chores and duties they had done together, and now Growler said his name. Coy liked it and now felt part of Growler's existence and life.

"As I am sure you know, I have a million or so questions, sir. Let's start with just one or two again," Coy spat out, while continuing to look around the shed yet with enough clarity and thought to elicit his thoughts to Growler.

"Okay, okay, but let's start with philosophical questions. This way I can test and find out who you are as well," Growler said with clarity.

Coy did not know how to respond and was confused by what philosophical questioning even meant. However, he did not want to show any kind of despondency or weakness. "That will work, sir, but you may have to start it off." Coy responded without even knowing how clever it was to deflect the questioning back to Growler. Coy looked over at Growler and caught him smiling. "Hey, what are you smiling about?"

Well, will you look at that?" Growler said as he pointed up and towards the south side wall.

"What?" Coy responded.

"That old sled hanging on that old two-by-four over there," Growler said.

"So, what's the big deal?" Coy retorted.

"See the words painted on the top of that old sled?" Growler went on.

"Sure, I think," Coy said, squinting. "I think it says Rosebud. Is that what it says?"

"Yes, that is what it says and apparently only Kane really knows." Growler laughed while responding.

Coy had no idea what that was all about.

"Hey, look over there up above that shelf with the old Evinrude oil can, right to the left of the window opening. Is that a belt or something?" Coy shouted with excitement.

"Yes, yes, I think it is. Let's find something for me to climb up there so we can take a look," Growler responded.

Coy noticed an old kitchen stool with a cut-off back next to the old decrepit John Deere B tractor, which was parked in the back of the shed.

"Hey, that should work." He proudly pointed at it for his working compadre.

"Yes, bring it over here," Growler said.

Coy stepped over an old tricycle, jumped over a pile of old life jackets, picked up the stool and sidestepped an old tire while finding his way to the stool. He looked over at Growler and found a more direct trek back over to the area where the potential belt was hanging on the wall. He placed the stool approximately where it needed to be for Growler to step up and take a look to see if the belt hanging on the nail would possibly work for their task at hand.

Growler leaned on Coy for support and stepped on the old stool. It worked, and he grabbed the belt and looked intently at it while quickly deducing its possibility. Growler grunted a bit in Coy's direction without any verbal communication. Coy knew what the grunt meant and followed behind. They made their way through the manmade obstacle course in the shed and walked out of the building. It was now time to block up the lawnmower and take a look to figure out and estimate the needs before too much more digging in the shed was to be done.

"I will pick up the right side of the mower, as the drain plug is on the left side. It is always the right thing to tip it opposite because if you don't, oil could possibly fill a cylinder and foul a plug when we restart the engine. From what I can see, there is probably not any decent or new plugs just sitting around in the shed," Growler said, while looking intently at Coy. "Then, set a block or two under there while I lift it up so we can take a look under the drive and blade area."

"Sounds good to me, sir," Coy replied, and complied all with one motion.

Coy appreciated the engine and oil and foul plug information and, to date, he realized that explanation was most likely the best elucidation of a situation on any subject that came out of Growler since they met, as he gave the potential problem and the solution all in one statement. Together they worked on the mower with smooth precision and, as each minute passed,

Coy's fondness for Growler grew. He had never met a grown-up man who treated him as a friend or helper or a compadre without any innuendos toward him being a kid. Coy felt like he was just another person to Growler.

Growler came around to Coy's side and lay down on the ground to get a good look under the mower. "This shouldn't be too bad. The drive belt popped off, and it looks to be okay. Another win for the team," he said with a succinct and clear thought and response process.

Coy's curiosity about Growler continued as the effort and conversation moved on. His mind was empty of trying to figure out the mystery and just wanted to be friends.

Let's see, we need a ¾ inch wrench to take off the blades, and it looks like a 9/16 inch to take off the guard," Growler said from under the mower, and as if only to himself.

Coy immediately spoke up. "I am sure the wrenches are on the bench. I will go take a look. Do you need any screwdrivers or pliers or anything else?"

Growler pulled himself about halfway from under the mower and turned his head so he could look right at Coy and responded with his distinctive raised right eyebrow glance. Coy knew when they played cards together, this was the signal for Coy to make his next move. "It sure is nice having you around, Coy," Growler said, as Coy was already to his feet and turning in the direction of the shed.

Coy stepped back without turning around and walked backward into the shed in utter amazement at the comment. It was as if Growler knew exactly what to say and when to say things and although Coy did not want it to be a distraction, it was.

The barn or shed cat meowed and bolted out from under the bench and scared the dickens out of Coy as he stepped backwards into the shed. However, not even that was enough to distract Coy from the moment he was having with Growler. He did a quick turn around and hit his left elbow on the side of the workbench, but his adrenaline was so high that even a knock to the funny bone in his left elbow was no bother, although it did hurt.

Coy was correct. He found the disorganized and scattered wrench set and found the wrenches Growler thought he needed and grabbed a flat head screwdriver, a Phillips head screwdriver, and a medium-sized crescent wrench along with a workbench rag. He walked back out to Growler. He laid the eighteen-by-eighteen-inch rag down on the half-gravel, half-grass front entrance of the shed and laid out the tools carefully for his friend and technician to go to work on the machine.

Growler looked at the tools and did not say a word, as there was chemistry between these two souls that did not need communication. Little did either one of them, so early in their relationship, realize it was based upon a life of need and discovery and not on words and actions.

Growler took a quick look under the unit and asked for the 9/16-inch wrench. Coy complied, grabbing the wrench and handing it to him.

"What is the first task?" Coy asked.

"Well, we need to take off the belt guard to uncover the belt drive, then we can inspect the drive to see if there is any damage that might have caused the belt to pop off," Growler responded with clear English.

Coy nodded, even though Growler was looking under the unit and they could not see each other. Coy knew his response was heard, even though it was not seen. In the world of communication, this was the most powerful form of communication as Growler explained to him time and time again for the rest of the summer adventure. The first example would be that Growler never spoke out loud when people were around. In fact, Coy did not know if Growler spoke to anyone else. Coy realized at that moment, communication did not have to be seen or heard and, in fact, could transcend time and presence.

"Got it. The nut finally let loose and is moving," Growler said. "Looks like the drive is okay, but maybe a shot of grease in the insert while we have the cover off and before we reinstall the belt would be a good idea. Hey, young man, did you see that grease gun hanging up on that nail to the left of the small entrance door in the shed?" Growler asked, while trying to look at Coy.

"Yes, yes, I did. I'll go get it, no problem," Coy responded enthusiastically. He felt an awareness and likeness with Growler as if he was looking at himself in the mirror fifty years or so in the future. Fifty years to a twelve-year-old was more than a lifetime and not thinkable, but Coy had a feeling.

He rose up from his knee as he was carefully watching Growler do the work under the mower, turned, and walked to the shed. He could not let this one time with Growler pass without asking the question that he wanted to ask him since he was in his pondering mode on Dock 1 an hour before. Coy asked while walking to the shed, looking right back at Growler as their eyes met. "Who do you see when you look in the mirror, Growler?" Coy uttered.

Somehow and from somewhere deep in Coy's soul, he had this understanding that often in life we asked only the important questions to other important people in our lives, in our thoughts, and rehashing time after we parted company. And unfortunately, often later when we did have a chance to get together with folks with whom we had relationships, we outright forgot what we said, asked, or inferred, so we stifled our thoughts and made poor assumptions of what we thought we had said. We often assumed we asked all the right things with the appropriate responses and conclusions.

Coy did not realize the wonderful God-given drive and ability to ask the questions when they needed to be asked that he had been given, and it was truly a natural way within his personality.

Growler pulled himself from under the mower and sat up and had a discerning look while starting his response with his broken half-German, half-Northern Minnesota Norwegian, then changed back to his perfect clear English. "I see many lives and many times... I see me then, when, where, and with whom, and I see myself as that twelve-year-old kid without the life that followed. I see every mistake, every order, every bad thing ever delivered right at me..."

He stopped and dropped the wrench and rag from his hand. His brow was covered with large beads of sweat. He looked right at Coy. Coy had never seen someone with that expression in his entire life. It was so deep and dark, like looking right at the moon, and the only thing visible was the darkness in between.

Coy discerned very quickly he had hit a note with Growler. He turned around and headed into the shed. "Hey, I found the grease gun. Give me a second as I need to find a stool or something, so I can reach it." Coy spoke up keenly with all the joy possible in the middle of a hellish moment.

"Very well, young man. You took me aback a bit there with that question." Growler spoke with his clear English. "Very well done, Coy, you jumped us right into the philosophy. I am not an armchair philosopher in any way. My thinking comes from life and experience. I can see you are as interesting as I deduced the first time our paths crossed this side of Heaven. I have watched and listened very carefully to you for the past few weeks. I knew there was and is something there." Growler stopped talking and paused for reflection.

"The evil men do lives after them. The good is often interred with their bones..." Growler said calmly and with perfect English and continued, "That Shakespeare was and is a pretty smart fellow." Growler responded with his broken language halfway through reciting Shakespeare, as if he was talking from two perspectives.

Coy did not know how to respond. The incongruity with Growler's speech and thought pattern would be a struggle for a seasoned college professor. Coy knew he had to just listen and let it happen and decipher as best as possible. He had no choice. He really did not even know what the word *philosophy* really meant. He let it go for a minute, as he found an old pail with a little dirt on the bottom of it, poured out the contents and tipped it over to stand on it to reach for the grease gun. He finished the task and started walking over toward Growler. He realized Growler was in another world and not present.

"Hey, hey, are you with me, man?" Coy spoke up with authority.

"Thoreau said something about the satisfaction of leaving the beaten path, and he intends to find it..." Growler was muttering, apparently in response to Coy, but more out to the world.

"What in the world does that all mean, and who is Thorward, or whoever it was you said had said that?" Coy spoke now standing near Growler.

"That is Thoreau, my son. He wrote an incredible little book many years ago about a place called Walden Pond. In fact, I also am looking for the Walden Pond in my life..." Growler, now speaking with perfect diction in English, stopped himself from continuing with his thought. It was as if he thought that he had gone too far.

Coy intently listened as Growler spoke, trying to hear every possible jewel of wisdom. He thought the old man looked worried and happy all at the same time. The moment was like when the fish only seemed to really hit and bite when the weather was coming in or when the lake was rough and maybe the extra attention helped the catching.

"Growler?" Coy began to speak, realizing he was getting comfortable with his name, well at least the name people called him. There was no response from the old man. Coy was hoping he had not offended him in any way.

But then the old man stood straight up and looked at Coy with his left eyebrow raised, and said, "Why did you call me Growler?"

"Isn't that your name?" Coy responded.

"My name is C. J. Stores..." Growler answered without completing the thought and name.

"If that is your name, why do people call you Growler?" Coy asked with a brave heart and hoped sincerely for a hint into the mystery.

"It is only a symbol of noise to me and to my ears," Growler responded. "Well, let's finish up this job and get this mower going again, so you can finish up the grass cutting on the back side of the house and the end piece behind Cabin 7," he continued with a broken tone.

"What? How come I am mowing now?" Coy asked.

"Well, you are the one causing the delay with all these questions and inquiries. Blessed is the man who has some congenial work, some occupation in which he can put his heart." Growler spoke with perfect English again. Lesson taught and learned.

He kneeled down and reached under the mower deck, and within just a few minutes the job was complete. They worked together like it was a partnership that had been there forever. They did not say another word until all the tools were put back in the shed. The mower was running with the blades moving, and all the actions of the machine were in order.

"Coy, you are a very interesting young man. I see much of me in you. I very much want the best for you and your future. Let's plan on going out to Jordan's Bay in the morning and pick up a couple for breakfast. It is so peaceful and important to me to go out there on Sunday mornings. I want to share and learn more with you. I will leave this thought with you: the real test to find whether your mission on earth is finished is if you're alive. It isn't." He calmly spoke with Coy, raised his left eyebrow, and without another word turned in the direction of Little Mora and started walking and left Coy with the mower running.

"Have a nice day," Coy said, but not loud enough for Growler to hear. He jumped up on the mower and went about the task of finishing up the mowing.

He completed the job about thirty minutes later. His shirt was soaking wet from sweat, but to Coy it was worth it. He had time to reminisce and really prepare his heart and mind for his next one-on-one encounter with this mystery man who he could now call a friend.

Coy remembered talking with Grandpa, telling him during a cribbage game that the key to staying young was to keep the blood flowing, and this definitely was one of those days that kept the blood flowing. Coy needed some alone time again and finishing up on the mowing would and did fit the bill. In that short period of time, Coy mowed perfectly the final bit to mow without even having to think about the how to, the where to, or any specifics. It was like not having to tell the mouth to chew—it just did.

A recent memory from school popped into Coy's mind during his mowing time, and it was an overwhelming memory from physical education class with Mr. Nelson the past fall. Mr. Nelson was also the basketball coach for the junior high and a former all-American collegiate basketball player from the University of Minnesota. He was one of Coy's favorite teachers at school. This guy was just plain a nice guy who knew just what to say and when to say it. Mr. Nelson started off with the class of both boys and girls and warmed up the class by giving a small portion of his history, teaching, and former and current sports accomplishments. He went on to teach the class that everyone thought they could be anything they wanted and all they had to do was want it and work for it.

Then he said, "The bleachers are full of All-Americans."

Coy remembered and noticed again hair was starting to sprout up from the top of his big toes and in other areas of his body. In that other area of his body, he noticed something happened when he was near attractive girls or even attractive young women, and the twinges felt different down below the belt once in a while. And of course, girls started looking a bit more like older women in body, and many of them thought cleaning up and putting a little makeup or something on was par for the course. Play-wrestling with Lisa, the neighbor down the street back home, wasn't quite the same as it was when they were nine years old and hanging on a jungle gym at school to see who would let go first.

But more importantly, differentiation of physical and mental talents started to really surface at this young adult stage. Coach Nelson knew exactly what to say and when to say it, and Coy on that fall morning heard it. During his time on the mower, Coy worked through his thoughts and really began to understand.

We all had something. It needed to be assessed honestly and worked on. Even though people had natural God-given talents, there was more to it than just saying, "I can do it." It took effort, a bunch of practice, luck, desire, and many other factors. Coy was starting to realize it took more and needed more than inner desire. It took that inner desire to be strong enough that action did not come from a want but just happened. It was a bit like finishing up mowing an area, and not even knowing how or when it was finished. He just got it done. The effort became effortless. Some days felt so long, and later you thought that time went by so fast and later you figured out you were in a zone when the days went quickly and time slowed down.

Coy looked over the freshly cut grass and the clean lines the mower left behind. He thought about the messy lines of Growler and the cleanness of a little trimming that might help.

He parked the mower in the shed and looked around, observing all the shelves and hooks full of equipment, nuts, bolts, half-built engines, piles of half-finished projects, and wondered how many half-finished All-Americans were left in the shed.

CHAPTER 36

One of the Boys

Coy realized as he took his shirt off that he had worked up a quite a sweat.

He even could smell a slight stench surrounding his persona. He decided to make a beeline to Dock 1 and take an afternoon resort bath.

He started toward Dock 1 and strolled nosily behind Cabin 2 and heard the radio in the window. This time it was a Johnny Horton song, and he knew the radio was on the KKIN station. He recognized Johnny because his dad and Uncle David from Hibbing played the album with this song in the living room after last year's Christmas dinner. Coy really liked Johnny Horton music. He sang along, "When it's springtime in Alaska I'll be six feet below..." He walked around the corner of Cabin 2 and the radio man said, "That was Johnny Horton. It is too bad he died way too young." Coy imagined and thought about dying way too young and how awful it was Johnny died young. However, he felt good about how his songs live on and were still being played.

He made his way to Dock 1 without even knowing how he got there. He decided to take a good run at it and jump off the end of the dock into the four-feet-deep water. The instant he hit the water; he was refreshed. He floated on this back for three or four minutes and just enjoyed the cool down. It was not much of a bath, more a refreshing dip. He jumped back onto the dock and lay down to dry off. It didn't take long for him to doze off. He enjoyed a refreshing afternoon siesta.

He woke up with a start, as three young ladies were on the shoreline and staring right out at him. He sat up and looked over and recognized them and said, "Well, hello, fine ladies. How are you all doing?"

They giggled, and Tess spoke up and told him again to make sure to come to the fish fry and campfire between Cabins 4 and 5 and to be there around 7 o'clock.

"Make sure you bring your Grandpa and your older friend you hang out with all the time," Ruby continued.

"I am not sure if I can speak up for them, but I will be there," Coy answered.

"See you later," they said in unison as they turned and started skipping and singing and humming while heading back to their family area.

"Okay, then," he responded loudly.

Coy knew it would be impossible to continue his rest now that he was awake. Besides, he had a very bad case of being afraid to miss out on anything all the time. He lived with a fear of missing out, and sleeping and resting was always a challenge, especially during the daytime hours. He was nearly dry anyway, so he decided to get up and head over to Little Mora and try to catch up with Grandpa or Growler and maybe play some kings on the corner or cribbage.

This time as he walked by Cabin 2, the radio was playing Jim Croce's "Time in a Bottle" song. Coy stopped and listened. He could not help but think of how beautiful the poetry of the lyrics was, and he thought it was very different from the "Bad, Bad Leroy Brown" song he had memorized. He looked over toward Little Mora once the song was over. Grandpa was on a lawn chair with his legs crossed, looking serene and rested. He did not see Growler, but knew he would be around there somewhere and spotted Growler stepping out of the two-holer behind Little Mora as he started walking back to where Grandpa was sitting.

Coy jumped over Chelsea Brook and was within earshot of Grandpa.

"Not too bad, kid. Three girls all taking a good look at you," Grandpa said.

"What? They were making sure we knew about the resort fish fry and campfire tonight and wanted to make sure we go," Coy retorted.

"Of course, Growler double cleaned up a pan full a couple of minutes ago for the fish fry. This is your first resort fish fry and you have three dates, not bad for a Pojken. You know what, we will make a man out of you yet," Grandpa continued.

Growler was grabbing another lawn chair and set it next to him by the time Grandpa finished up with that comment. He looked at Coy and smiled as he sat down. Coy understood the non-verbal communication as "I agree with him, but do not take him too seriously."

"You, too, huh?" Coy said, while looking at Growler. "Hey, do you want to play a game of cards?"

Growler sat up from the chair and gave Coy a lifted-up eyebrow stare and made a few steps to the screen door. He looked again at Coy, and Coy knew the answer was yes. Pretzel as usual, as if by instinctual desire, was lying down on the ground at Grandpa's left side. Grandpa stared out in the direction of the lake as he sat relaxed and petted him. Pretzel had a warm and friendly personality and always responded with a smile and wagging tail.

Coy made his way to the cabin. Growler had the cribbage board out and the cards ready. They played three games, and Growler won two. Growler never said a word the entire time they played. Coy always double-checked Growler's count and never once found an error. Nothing was said during the hour of play but much was communicated. Coy was growing very fond of Growler. Growler was growing very fond of Coy.

After they were done playing, Growler picked up the board and hung it up on the nail on the wall. Coy put the cards away on the small shelf next to the ice box. They walked out of the cabin together, and they found Grandpa had dozed off in the chair. It was a very comfortable temperature in the shade, and the light breeze from the northern wind blowing in from the lake was soothing. Coy understood. He sat down on one of the tree stumps. They sat together for another half an hour or so until around five o'clock.

Grandpa awakened. He broke the silence and said, "Well, maybe we should divide up and look over the resort and meet up down at Cabin 4 in an hour or so. Make sure you bring along those fish," he said, looking Growler's way.

All of them nodded in agreement and went their separate ways. Coy felt like one of the boys.

Coy heard kids playing over by the fish house and figured out it was Jimmy and Gary chasing each other around. Knowing they would be leaving the next day, he thought he had better get over there and fulfill a promise of playing with them. It was always fun to be one of the boys. Coy ran over and joined in the chasing game with Jimmy and Gary. He looked over at Grandpa and Growler over by Little Mora and felt like one of the boys.

One Lifetime Is Not Enough!

CHAPTER 37

Resort Fish Fry and Campfire

Grandpa, Growler, and Coy were back at Little Mora around 6 o'clock.

They were sitting on the chairs right outside the cabin together. Coy was filled with anticipation for the fish fry and campfire this evening. He was thinking about how it all would go, as it was going to be the first time together with these folks along with Grandpa and Growler.

"Get your singing voices ready, boys. There is a good chance we will sit around the fire and sing. Those cabins are filled with musical people," Grandpa said, breaking the silence while looking at Growler, and then he turned to Coy with his customary slightly devilish smirk.

Coy got it this time and responded, "I really like music, but I really don't like my voice and get really nervous singing around people."

"Don't worry, Coy, you'll be fine," Grandpa responded, while looking away from Coy.

Coy looked over at Growler, and Growler responded with his usual Spock eyebrow lift. Coy always took that as, "See, I told you so," or "Hey, I really know what you are thinking."

Whatever it meant, Coy was apprehensive about possibly having to sing with people, so he gave a raised eyebrow look back in response.

"I am going to check on the fish house one more time and see you guys later." Coy got up and started walking away. He passed by Growler and patted the shoulder of the old man warmly.

"Remember, your smell might not be too bad tonight, but there is always a chance that your stench will carry the moment," Grandpa said, chuckling as Coy walked away. They all laughed out loud. Coy made a few steps and turned around and saw that both Grandpa and Growler had gotten up and were heading different directions.

Coy made it over to the fish house, and even though there had been some fish cleaning, he found the fish house clean and in good order. However, he pumped the well and took the hose and did another quick spray around, and as he did, he saw Gary and Jimmy kicking around the soccer ball over behind Cabins 5 and 6.

He finished up and tied the hose up around the pump and walked over to see if he could jump into the game with the boys. He looked around and noticed Tess and the girls were talking and goofing around between Cabins 4 and 5. He approached Gary and Jimmy. The ball came his way. He decided to play and jumped into the action. They played a mock game of kicking it around until someone missed their target. The girls spotted Coy and the boys and immediately started going in their direction. Of course, a boys versus the girls game started up, and the girls won once again. Coy was getting a little tired of losing to girls. But losing to Tess was not a bad thing. He always enjoyed seeing Tess smile.

Ruby spoke up and told the group that they better get over to the fish fry after playing for twenty minutes or so. They finished up and all together started walking to the front of Cabin 4. As they made their way there, the girls went one way and the boys another. Coy stood in front of the Cabin 4 and estimated that there were about fifteen adults sitting and standing and talking and laughing. The crowd of people was either around the picnic table or on lawn chairs, and a couple of people were down by the fire pit located between the picnic table and the lakeshore.

Growler was sitting on one of the old stumps by the fire pit, working the wood around it and stoking the newly lit fire. Grandpa was sitting in one of the lawn chairs to the side of the picnic table and in conversation with El's grandfather and one of Tess's uncles, who were both sitting in lawn chairs next to him.

El's mother and one of Tess's aunts came out of their respective cabins with bowls of freshly fried fish in one hand and salads and table settings in the other. Ruby, Molly, and Tess jumped right in behind them and were helping by bringing other fixings. The table had utensils, plates, and accompaniments already on it, and it looked like things were in order. Gary and Jimmy were already down on the Cabin 5 dock, throwing rocks in the water.

Coy felt like he had just entered the Twilight Zone or somewhere. He realized this was one of those moments where he wanted to be alone and within the group of people at the same time. He wanted to be anonymous, yet acknowledged and recognized. He decided to sit down on the edge of the bench of the picnic table on the opposite end from Grandpa. El came over and sat on the other side of the table.

"How you are doing, Coy?" El asked.

"Okay," Coy responded.

"Don't worry, my friend; you will be okay anyway," El responded.

"What, what did you say?" Coy asked.

"Well, I know you. We are a quite a bit alike. You just want to observe and not be observed, right?" El asked.

"Well, I guess so, whatever that all means," Coy responded.

El's grandmother spoke up loud enough for the group to hear and said,

"Daddy, it is time to say grace."

El's grandfather immediately stood up by Grandpa and took off his old worn Cubs baseball cap and put his hands together. Everyone immediately stopped what they were doing and stood and came to attention.

"Praise God, praise Jesus, and praise the Holy Spirit. Glory to Thy name. Thank You for life. Thank You for friends, family, and fellowship. Bless the hands who prepared the meal, and bless our time together because, after all, we are but one with You, oh dear Lord. Amen." He finished and there was a splatter of applause, and then the noise of conversation continued.

Someone said, "Hey, can you hear the loons? Doesn't that sound beautiful?"

El's uncle, who was sitting next to Growler by the fire, started playing a guitar. He fiddled around and warmed up a bit and started singing— *"Put your hand in the hand of the man from Galilee."*

By the time he finished singing the first verse, several people were singing along. He started the first verse again and the singing was as if one voice. Coy looked around and noticed the whole group of people settled down. He even felt brave enough to sing along. He stumbled along and the words amazed him while he listened and sang carefully. He got up to move closer and El was right next to him singing. They looked at each other and smiled.

The fish fry was excellent. Coy thought it was as if Mom was there, taking care of him, and it was really nice to eat some good food. He could feel Mom and missed her, but he knew he was where he was supposed to be. Later, as he lay down to sleep, he remembered the prayer and could not stop thinking about the "being one together" statement, then he started humming, "Put your hand in the hand of the man from Galilee."

CHAPTER 38

Jordan's Bay Part Three – I Love you like a Tomato

A couple of days later, it was Sunday morning, July 15, 1973. Coy was thrilled to have the opportunity to go out to Jordan's Bay with Growler. Coy was prepared, and he had been in Little Mora four times reading and studying from Growler's book.

The threads holding the mystery of Growler were becoming conspicuous. Coy now knew Growler at a different level and understood that he had a very interesting life. The exposed story showed a man who tried desperately to take control of his life at the same time not desiring or maybe not having the ability to ask for help. Coy thought Growler had lived a very lonely existence, knowing that he really had no comprehension or understanding of being lonely. Coy would finish his study and reading from Growler's book with new perspective every time. However, there was one subject that stood out to Coy. It was where Growler wrote he could not let any family member know he was alive, and the government made sure that was clear by even informing his family he had been killed in service.

Growler wrote in frustration as his past life was dead to those in his life he had ever loved or who loved him. Coy remembered reading a section where Growler described going to the cemetery in his hometown of Thief River Falls secretly and finding his own gravesite and how he studied the gravesite and pondered if he was buried there already. After all, eyes of the dead could no longer see.

Coy prepared for Jordan's Bay and reminisced how fun and inspiring the moment felt, especially seeing a small smile on Growler's face at the singalong. However, Sunday morning could not come fast enough for Coy. He felt ready for anything and based upon the changes and bonding gradually happening in his relationship with Growler, his level of anticipation was reaching a zenith.

Once again, they both woke up early, went about some chores, and planned on meeting shortly after 8 a.m. at Dock 1. Neither of them wore watches. Over the few weeks, Coy knew the feel of 8 a.m. It felt different from 5, or 6, or 7 a.m. It was warmer, and the morning dew was close to being burnt away. The 8 a.m. feel became more obvious each day to Coy.

Growler came from behind Cabin 2, which was the more direct path from Little Mora. Coy was walking along the shoreline in front of Cabin 2. He had just filled a half milk carton, which doubled for the home of the worms they would be using as bait. They met almost simultaneously at Dock 1 and acknowledged each other with quick smirky grins. They walked side by side down the dock as Growler jumped into the front of the fourteen-foot Lund boat. He checked for life jackets, oars, and fishing poles. He began to untie to rope from the dock and held the boat tight to the dock as Coy jumped in the back of the boat. He lifted up the gas can to make sure there was gas, nudged the gas line connected to the seven-and-a-half Mercury motor and, with a smooth and seasoned hand, pulled the back rope attached to the dock holding the boat to the dock post. He held the boat to the dock and glanced at Growler to make sure they were ready to launch. Once again, their eyes met and, with an unspoken bond, acknowledged the time was right.

Coy knew the water depth at Dock 1 was about a foot too shallow to lower the motor all the way down immediately, so he left the motor up one notch until the boat was at least twenty-five or so feet out from the dock. In addition, Dock 1 was located so far to the east side of the shoreline that it was within reach of the lily pads and weeds from the east shore line, which grew out more each summer day. Therefore, besides going straight out north from the dock, it was also necessary to veer off to the west a bit to be directly out from Dock 2, where the water was at least six feet deep.

Coy lowered the motor down to its last position when it was appropriate, and they were ready to make their trip out to the midpoint of the main area of the lake. They would make a gradual directional change due west and into Jordan's Bay. Like Grandpa would say occasionally when they were out together fishing outside of Jordan's Bay, "It sure is nice to stay east of Eden." Coy did not know what that meant, but it was stuck in his mind.

The entrance into Jordan's Bay became narrower and weedier even during the few weeks Coy had been at the resort. The nice summer weather and weed growth was soaring. Entering the narrow passageway into Jordan's Bay would take past experience and additional care to watch where the lake bottom was shallow, where the motor would not be in danger of hitting rocks or getting caught up in the muck of the bottom and messed up in weeds. With Growler's help and guidance and working together, they were able to get the boat through the narrow passageway smoothly. And this morning, they made it look easy. Coy practiced many times in his mind to not show even one bit of weakness in front of Growler or Grandpa when he had the chance to run the motor and captain lake adventures. Coy felt it was doubly important not to show weakness when going into the Jordan's Bay with Growler.

Growler pointed over to the familiar location in the southwest corner of the bay where there was a nice windbreak from the tree-lined shore. It was also a prime location for fishing. The lily pads were the big, flowering type, and they were thick. Coy thought the lily pads looked strong enough that he might even be able to walk on them. They positioned the boat close to the area where the invisible line of the river crossing across the lake actually exited at the southwest shoreline where the hill ended. The Mississippi River was less than two miles south of Lake Esquagamah. The small tributary creek meandered through the low swamp-like ground and when the water was high, it could be traveled in a small rowboat for over five miles before it entered the mighty Mississippi. Three miles down the gravel road from the resort entrance, there was a bridge crossing this small creek where bullhead fishing was unbelievable. Often when the lake was just not producing, vacationers would head there and at least have some fun fishing for bullies. When cleaned and fried up right, even Coy had to admit, a bullhead did not taste too bad.

The water this morning was serene and calm. There wasn't a wave in the bay except the waves the boat had generated. Out on the main body of the lake, the water was a little choppy from the mild morning wind. It was as if they entered a whole new world when they entered the bay. Communication was abounding and present between these two souls with no spoken word. The boat magically ended up almost to within a foot of the spot they had been just a week before. Growler enjoyed being out on the lake on Sunday mornings. It was his refreshment. Frankly, Coy enjoyed it just as much. The little white church building could be easily seen from this location, and the sounds of the church bell could be heard loud and clear. The music from the church could be heard as if this location was a mere extension of the church. The voices from the church could be heard but were muffled; reactions and responses were obvious and could be felt. The Sunday service was an hour away. It was around 9 a.m. as the anglers dropped the boat's anchor at the exact and appropriate location in Jordan's Bay.

The boat stopped as the waves from the boat settled into the serene water. Coy looked across the bay towards the narrow passageway and thought it looked so pleasant and revealing. He wanted to step out of the boat and walk on water right back through the passageway to prove a point. He even thought that if he did sink into the water, it could not have been more than four or five feet deep, and maybe he would be able to make it somehow anyway.

However, he was a little scared of water and didn't want to even think about trying to do it.

Coy handed the worm carton to Growler. He was not quite ready to fish yet and wanted to settle into the surroundings. The weather was less humid this morning than the last time they were out there together; it was around seventy degrees. It was a perfect northern Minnesota summer morning with a clear sky, a nice morning breeze, and the perfect location. Even with all in order, fishing was not on Coy's mind or agenda. The only thing on his mind was to really get to know

Growler better this morning and ask some prepared questions. God set up the environment with perfection, now it was up to Coy to grab ahold of the moment.

Growler grabbed the worm carton. Their eyes met, and Coy took a good deep look. Coy estimated Growler was somewhere around sixty years old. Coy saw him as pretty fit for a man his age. Anyone over twenty years old was old to Coy. Growler's shirt looked like it was part of his personality and went exactly where a shirt was supposed to be at all times. His face was broad and craggy from the sun with morning salty whiskers and a lower jaw that protruded slightly, making him look prouder than he must have felt. He wore an old linen baseball cap from Crystal Sugar. With his protruding lower jaw, he always seemed to be grinning, like a dolphin. His expression had a way of making people trust him, and Coy did.

There did not seem to be any dull routines about Growler based on Coy's discernment over the past four weeks of living, eating, fishing, playing cards, doing chores, sitting silently at the nightly resort campfires, and even sitting together in the two-holer. They sat there, scratched themselves and farted, and from this freedom came laughter- roars of laughter. It was like Coy and Growler lived as if all the days of the world were still to come. Coy thought that even though they had only met a few weeks before, he wanted to see and know Growler as a friend.

Growler was graying and aging. His pants seemed loose and in a state of weary acceptance. He looked like a man who had accepted who he was now and who he would always be, a man with enormous weight in his shoes in a world of mechanical, made-up laughter where he was the only one who knew the true engine behind the humor. His earned dark-complexioned face took on the serious expressionlessness of a man who was nearly always alone and happy with it all without having to smile.

The silence was broken. Growler brought consciousness to the moment or, rather, nudged the dozing unconsciousness.

"Kid, I never been anywhere I wasn't shipped to without a rifle." Growler spoke with his half-broken, sputtered style.

"What?" Coy responded.

"Also, let's make a pact to be genuine this morning," Growler continued. He lifted his left eyebrow with his nonverbal response in Coy's direction. Coy loved the look and got it. "I do want to be real, Coy, but my wounds often feel like they are under old bandages. I have grown more used to the bandages than the wounds that were meant to be healed." Growler spoke with perfect clear diction.

They looked away from each other across the bay simultaneously. The water looked like diamonds from the sunlight dancing across the water. They stared together at the nimble movements of the slight water waves and sunlight reflections. It was a necessary distraction for them both, as both of their heads were filled with a cacophony of crashing waves and thoughts- one young, and one older- but both one life. Looking back later, Coy remembered this day was just the right temperature, and the water had just the right serenity. The light and reflection of the sun danced perfectly that morning at just the right time and place.

The serenity of the moment gave Growler a surge of warmth unlike anything he had ever felt before. His lifetime of thoughts began to spill out in full sentences. He was like a bewildered bee, confused by too many flowers while bouncing from sweet flower to another.

Growler had an obvious buildup of a life of thoughts. However, it happened; sometime during the previous three or four weeks of Growler spending time with Coy, he realized he had spent a great deal of his life hiding from life, and the rest of the time he thought he went unnoticed.

Coy could not have spoken even if he wanted. He listened. Growler had years of memories and a life to share. Coy was a dry sponge when they entered the narrow passageway into Jordan's Bay on that summer morning.

He became a different person hearing another man's life story and, for several hours and even a week later and maybe for the rest of his life, became a fully wet sponge of thought. He had so much respect for this older man and felt a warmth for him that could be felt only for one who was not perfect and therefore was not a target for hatred, only love—an unexplainable love. Growler discerned the moment.

Growler was looking at his life, his dead life, his young life, his missing life, his only life, and he didn't want to look anymore. He ended his diatribe with, "Coy, one lifetime is not enough!" Then, he just stopped talking.

During this whole time, the bells from the church had rung and together, they had caught and kept about a dozen perfectly sized bluegill sunfish. Coy grabbed the fish basket hanging off the left side of the boat at the same time Growler lifted the anchor and cleaned the mud and weeds off of it then gently set it down in the boat. It took one pull, and the motor started. Together, they exited the narrow passageway as carefully as they entered, going out of Jordan's Bay into the main body of water and started their way back to Dock 1.

They were within twenty-five feet from the dock, and Coy knew Growler would change back to the Growler everyone else saw from his outward appearance and decided to ask one last question. "Please, Growler, will you give me one more thing to think about?"

"Things that happen before you are born still affect you. And people who come before your time affect you as well where we spend so much time and effort. We often think they began with our arrival. That is not true." Growler clearly spoke with conviction. These were the last spoken words Coy would hear from Growler for a week.

Coy stood up in the boat to get ready to step out onto the dock, pondering in his mind to direct his next move. His mind was filled with something his mother told him about her mother the morning she came up to his bedroom and tearfully told him grandma passed away.

"Coy, Grandmama had a tough exterior, and you often saw her directing and leading something at the farm or yelling at Grandpa... please do not judge her, Coy. Love her like I have always—Love her like a tomato... She had a tough skin but was soft on the inside. Look at the inside, Coy, always look at the inside." A tear fell from Coy's eyes as he remembered how important his mother was to him.

Coy tied up the boat and jumped up onto the dock. He turned and looked out at the lake and as he did, one of the loons popped out of the water about 100 yards off shore and sang its beautiful tune.

Coy smiled and silently recited, "Growler, I love you like a tomato. A tough skin on the outside and all soft inside."

CHAPTER 39

Saying Goodbye to El

Coy was looking across the water, standing on the end of Dock 1 in a zone.

Growler untied the fish basket from the side of the boat and headed right to the fish house immediately after they docked the boat. When Coy turned around, Growler was already near the boat access ramp and halfway to the fish house. He also needed alone time and did not signal for Coy to accompany or help him. He moved on and walked away alone.

Coy looked farther down the shoreline and saw El and his family in front of their cabin, sitting around the picnic table eating lunch. Coy decided to walk over there, knowing they were preparing to leave some time later this day.

As he got close, he said, "Hi everyone, what a beautiful day."

Several of them looked up, and El answered, "Hey, it's Coy. Hi, buddy, how are you doing this morning?"

Coy answered, "Just fine. Are you guys getting ready to head home?"

"Yes, we are, young man," El's mother responded from the side of the cabin, while carrying a plate of sandwiches. "Would you like to break bread with us?"

Coy did not quite understand that "break bread" comment, but he did remember the last time he had one of her sandwiches, and it was very good.

"Yes, that would be delightful," he respectfully accepted.

"Well, we're cleaning out the ice box, and there's a bunch of different selections. But I remember this would fit your taste buds, and I think the best we have to offer. Young man, always offer your guest your best," she said.

Coy received the sandwich and that bit of wisdom carried on in him for the rest of his life.

She set the plate down on the table, and everyone became silent. She went on to pray for the meal, family, friends, foes, and the world, and asked for blessings.

Coy sat down next to El. They had a nice conversation and El told him he really liked him and wished him all the best in his life and hoped someday they would meet up again. After the meal, Coy thanked all of them, stood up with El, and they embraced in a warm hug.

"Goodbye, buddy," Coy said while hugging El. He turned and starting walking toward Cabin 4. It was time to see when those folks were leaving as well.

CHAPTER 40

Saying Goodbye to Tess

Tess's family was in Cabin 4.

Coy remembered Grandpa mentioned the night before at the fire that all the cabins would be turning over in the next couple of days. Coy wanted to make sure he saw Tess one more time. Down deep in a place he could not explain, there was a desire to make sure he looked right at her and etched her presence into his mind.

The new incoming vacationers for Cabin 4 were not going to come in until Tuesday morning and Grandpa asked Tess's family if they wanted to stay another night. They accepted. Coy looked down by the lake and the dock and saw the girls there. Tess was sitting on the edge of the fallen tree that hung over the water. Coy made his way down there and sat next to her.

"Hi," was all he could muster.

Oh, hi," she responded.

"I understand you guys are staying another night; I wanted to make sure I had a chance to see you and say goodbye in case you took off early or something," Coy said.

"Well, that sure is nice of you," she responded.

"Tess, will you look me right in my eyes?" Coy asked.

"Sure, but why?" she responded.

"Nothing much, well... I do not know what I should say except I really want to remember you. People come and go so fast. People die, people are born, people come across our paths and just in case I never see you again, I never want to forget you," he said.

Tess looked him directly in his eyes and said, "I never want to forget you, either."

The look was for only a few seconds, but Coy knew it was enough for a lifetime.

CHAPTER 41

One Final Reading

Coy knew Grandpa and Growler were busy with chores so during an afternoon break a few days later, he made his way into Little Mora. He also knew his time at the resort was coming to an end, and he wanted one final reading of the book if possible. With all the goings on the past couple of weeks and the hunger for unanswerable questions, his thought process was exploding in his mind. In a couple of days, he would go out into Jordan's Bay for the last time with Growler before he went back to his real world with his family. He wanted to see if there was one more treasure God wanted him to find or one more piece of evidence to help him solve the Growler mystery.

He made his way stealthily to the lampstand and decided to page through the book as if he was in preparation for a final exam. However, the twisted plot turned a notch when he looked down on the shelf of the lampstand and found two books. His curiosity was on high alert, so he put down the brown book and reached for the other book. It was a Bible.

He started leafing through it and found lots of notes written along the edges of the pages along with many loose pages and separate note pages every once in a while. Coy went to the front cover to see if the owner's name was written on it anywhere. It was not. He went to the back cover of the book to see if anything was written there and there was. It was fresh and new. Coy discerned it had been written on the back cover recently. He continued to leaf through the Bible, and he realized every once in a while, there was written on the bottom of several pages: *One lifetime is not enough.*

Coy turned to the last page of the Bible and as he did, a small piece of paper fell out and onto the floor. He set the Bible down on the bed and picked up the paper. The paper looked to be ripped out of a school binder page, and Coy thought about when Growler would have written what was on the paper, which was – *Please Lord, take away my masochistic delight in confronting uncomfortable truths.* Coy read it several times in an attempt to try to understand, but nothing came to his mind. He did not know what masochistic meant. He felt like the young boy he was when he came to the resort.

There was no illusion that the notes and pieces of paper were written at different times and with different pencils or pens. It delighted Coy to think about where in the world Growler was when he put the words down on paper and what he was reading.

Coy read out loud what was written near the end of the book. "The Lord has poured water over me like a deluge of a clean pure river."

He turned to the back cover of the book and etched what was written in his mind for a lifelong memory.

He made sure all the loose papers were carefully in place in the precious book, wrapped the band around it, and neatly put both of the books back in their place on the shelf of the lampstand.

He did not open the other book at all.
Coy prayed before he left the room.
"I pray for him, Lord. Help him find the life You want for him, because if one life is not enough, make it enough, Lord."
Coy was crying by the time he said Lord.

CHAPTER 42

Jordan's Bay Part Three - More Than a Murmur

Coy and Growler were out to the time-honored Sunday morning Jordan's Bay fishing spot one week later. "Growler, what do you want from God?" Coy asked, the second he turned the motor off.

Growler wanted desperately to answer. He had deep wounds. He was an expert and trained killer. He felt through all his killings that he also killed his own life. Every time he killed; it took a spark of life from him. Killing enemies doesn't make killing good.

Growler answered, "I no longer have any more life to give or take. I know you have been reading my book. I left my book out on purpose for some reason for someone to find. You are the only person ever in my life who wanted to read my book. I left my Bible out and I know you also read from it. Thank you.

"Coy, welcome aboard. For thousands of years, even before Homer's concave ships set sail for Troy, there were men with wrinkles around their mouths and rainy November hearts. Men whose nature led them sooner or later to look with interest into the black hole of a pistol barrel. Men who longed for desperate solutions and who always sensed then it was time to make an exit." Growler had so much to say his mouth was almost foaming like a volcano ready to explode.

Coy tried desperately to follow along, but it was like Growler was speaking babble. Then all of a sudden, he stopped talking, just like a radio stopping if someone bumps it off the window sill.

CHAPTER 43

Ending with Beginning

Growler was in such a condition he could no longer be identified with pronouns. He was only an object. His stare could turn the sun ice cold as if he was a direct descendant of the first murderer, Cain.

Over a lifetime, Growler had learned the only way to get away with death was to continually step within an inch of it. Life was to be taken, not given. The young man, of course, did not have the lifetime of experience that was being shattered this morning and sat there speechless and motionless but with serenity. He looked directly into the old man's bloodshot, well-traveled, deep, bottomless, mossy eyes. The moment was like a wild dream sequence in which danger was all around and the hero or the villain was frozen and could not move or even have the ability to move a muscle to retreat from the danger. The motionless, spine-chilling moment froze time.

Growler had faded eyes- eyes the color of swamp spume, and moss- eyes nobody else in the entire world would care to look out from. The moment silenced everything around them. Life was so quiet, even a drop of water falling into an ocean would have been heard. Coy could feel and hear his fingernails growing. The sudden feel of the cool wind blowing across the lake was all that was needed for the feeling that his teeth were burning. Unrecognizable senses and feelings were surfacing.

If Growler's eyes had the ability to speak, each eye could carry a conversation over an entire sports stadium of rabid fans screaming for no other reason than for desperate hope of attention. The irony of timeless stoicism was deeply embedded within those eyes and along with the deep, sagging circles directly under his eyes, he looked so stricken; it was like Jesus had taken a swing at him. The weight of life was upon him, so overwhelming, with the realization that his weary struggle of a loyal, stoic life might be at its end and outlived. He had outlived his purpose.

Silence was broken.

"Do you believe? Why? Who are you?"

Growler broke the silence and asked the young man as if interrogating. The timbre of his voice reflection was clear as he spat out seven words with his unusual well-traveled, practiced, and disturbing sputter. Growler had a way of speaking softly and loudly at the same time.

Coy knew his winsome smile would not shatter the strain of the moment and he remained dour. There was an eternal lifetime of built-up, covered-up anger that could not and would not be squelched with every intention within Growler. Even though his worn-out face and gestures looked more exhausted than earned from a close proximity, there was effervescent intention. Coy stared right into the man's eyes, eyes with the feel and color that men and women take up the sword to follow, the eyes nobody else sees. Coy remained serene, albeit scared beyond comprehension to the point of losing control of his feelings. Still, Coy perceived a sense of compassion.

Buttons he did not even know were present within his young heart thought process were being pushed. Coy had a hot, uneasy, helpless feeling coming over him, like being inside the belly of an enormous moth near a hot fire. His learning and desire to understand gave him surviving and enlightening thoughts, given from an unknown hollow.

Coy, at this exact moment, had compassion a young man could not obtain until kindness had filled him after an entire life of compassion hunting. He had peace, somehow and some way, right at this moment of truth with divine providence. Coy did not have time to think and if he did, he surely would not be able to identify the depth of the ache happening. It was like he had a blister on his instep and a gnat in his eye at the same time. He was starting to sense his total loss of being able to breathe. This was one of those surreal moments in time, like gazing over a majestic mountain view, speechless because of the mere unknowing feeling of not being able to describe the overwhelming flow of sensations and emotions.

Too many thoughts at once raced through his mind, like eating an entire box of chocolates just out of spite, without tasting the goodness. He had no time for reasoning and thinking. What would happen would happen as a poor or good habit, depending on the one's point of view. Coy's mouth was so dry even a sponge of vinegar would not satisfy. Whatever he could do or say was from the real purposed person within and, in no way, could have been rehearsed or engineered. The hesitation felt like eternity yet long enough. He was given the strength to respond. He had one simple and stirring response from a depth so deep it was past the inner workings of his own heart.

Coy began chanting clearly and without stumble, "Jesus loves me! This I know, for the Bible tells me so. Little ones to

Him belong; they are weak, but He is strong. Yes, Jesus loves me! Yes, Jesus loves me! Yes, Jesus loves me! The Bible tells me soooo." He sang it out with a youthful tone and with tears of joy and fear, just as it was supposed to be sung.

The moment climaxed like a small pebble landing in the center of a perfectly serene body of water, and the ripples became the only defining purpose. The old man's heart, figuratively and with spirit, left his chest and landed at his feet with a bounce, simultaneously with the loss of purpose. His strong grip on the .357 magnum revolver began to shake; his grip collapsed, and the gun fell to the bottom of the boat. His eyes welled from a dry source of forevermore. A marvel within the miracle of realization was happening between these two souls.

Growler did not cry. He did not even have one bead of sweat. He began to speak with pure and clear diction within a second of the collapse. Life hidden with grief had risen and grabbed hold of his heart. His soul was ambushed with emotions, and his lips began to tremble. He was swept into the current of all the potential loss of time. The devil had been fought, no holds barred, boots a-kicking and eye-gouging permitted. The old man was duly marked and scarred but survived.

"Jesus loves me, this I know, for the Bible tells me sooo..." the old man began to chant. "The best answer ever given, son. Life is not what just happens!" Growler said clearly as he looked intently into the eyes of the young man, with all intention of reaching the soul. The old man became young as if reborn before Coy's sight. His ears were ringing from the past as he could hear his first drill sergeant enter his soul when they were standing nose-to-nose some forty-plus years earlier. "All men die, few men ever really live. After all, you can't change Jesus, for Christ's sake!" Growler hesitated a moment and then continued, "Young man, Winston Churchill once said the most difficult moments and things in life so often can be described by one word." He paused for reflection and looked across the water, then said,

"Jesus."

Growler understood. One life is not enough!

Silence was broken when Coy said, "I love you, and I don't even know why."

"I recently left my Bible out for you also to find and read and you did. Thank you." Growler softly spoke as he took the book and the Bible out from under his overcoat. Growler handed his precious Bible to Coy and told him it was now his, and to read it cover to cover and when finished, read it again and again. "I wrote something on the back cover for you to remember me by."

Coy politely accepted it and thanked him with a nonverbal yet very loud response of thank you.

"Now I know with all my heart and soul that Jesus loves me. Nothing in or of this world matters. Coy, you showed me," Growler said, looking right in the young man's eyes.

Coy looked right back at Growler's beautiful, vibrant, mossy eyes and said, "I know what it written on the back cover of your memoir book and your Bible."

Coy softly recited the precious words written on the back covers without even looking at the back cover of either book. Growler smiled. He handed the Bible back to Growler with a wide, tearful, promising smile and said, "This is your life. Keep reading and writing."

CHAPTER 44

Ten Years Later – AMEN!

Coy had over ten years to find understanding and thoughts of Growler from their experience together. His precious memory always brought him close to God and Christ. He remembered the facts of Growler's life were so hidden in his early life where the seeds of a tragedy were much deeper than anyone could comprehend as if his life was lived in another world and spoken in another language. From afar, the impression was one of haunting loneliness anonymity, and mystery. But if anyone would have known the real Growler at all, it was Coy. At least that was what he thought and hoped.

Coy felt the burden of the moment. He knew he had to tell a truthful story—at least a glimpse.

Growler was always an enigma to Coy but in reality, it was the thought of Growler which was the enigma. Growler was just one life. Coy decided it was time to walk into the sanctuary and counted twelve people in the small church besides the pastor, who was sitting with his wife and three daughters. Everyone there were the exact folks God wanted present.

The pastor stood up and walked to the pulpit stand centered in the church right behind the small table that had the simple box holding the remains of Growler. There were three vases filled with flowers right behind the box. The pastor asked all present to pick up the hymnals and go to page seven. The piano started playing, and they sang the hymn, "I Love to Tell the Story". Coy knew every word and sang out with tearful joy. His heart was filled with awe and anticipation as he stood up once the pastor finished the prayer. The pastor waved for him to come up and speak.

"If you do good to but one, one life is not enough" was the last thing Coy wrote down on the well-prepared, ten-page eulogy he had finished the night before he left his dear wife and son. However, God did not want him to speak anything well-prepared. He walked up to the front of the church. The pastor waited for him at the pulpit and they shook hands. When the pastor started walking away, Coy warmly brushed the pastor's forearm. Their eyes met, and communication was abounding. Coy handed the pastor the envelope only Coy had seen, and said, "Please read what is inside this envelope before I start with the eulogy."

Coy picked up the pastor's guitar on the stand to the left of pulpit. He sat, put his notes and the small worn brown book down, along with his Bible, and put on the guitar strap around his neck then looked up and noticed that the sanctuary had now filled with people.

Coy enjoyed playing a the guitar, but did not play very well. He was able to strum a few licks and found a few chords when he concentrated. He prayed briefly and privately with hope that God would provide the skill this morning. He then said,

"The spoken word of God is what gives us one life. A glimpse of Christ is all we need." During that brief moment the pastor and his wife opened the envelope and read the enlightened words on the paper inside. They read together from the formal piece of paper that had staggered Coy earlier. The moment of revelation shook them to their cores. The pastor and his wife held each other tightly and were crying. Their three daughters were looking at them intently with love and bewilderment in their young eyes.

Coy looked at them, slowed his pace, took a deep breath, and smiled to give comfort. God had given him inner strength he did not know was there. Coy strummed a few notes and chords and started singing a poem he had memorized and found in Growler's book.

> Cold, cold day. Hills of green. Trees to hold His majesty. Crown of many thorns. Wine of bitter sour. Jesus, Lord of all in His holiest hour.
>
> A glimpse of Christ is all I need, to fill me up to set me free. Jesus gave His holy life to give me a chance to see... A glimpse of Christ.
>
> Songs of praise. Life of gold. Angel of mercy fills my soul. I see it and I cry, fall down to my knees. See a little God, now I cannot deny.
>
> A glimpse of Christ is all I need to fill me up to set me free. Jesus gave His holy life to give me a chance to see... A glimpse of Christ.

A glimpse of Christ is what I need to fill me up to set me free. Jesus gave His holy life to give me a chance to see... A glimpse of Christ.

Coy finished, and his eyes were swollen and full of tears. He closed his eyes and kept his head down for a moment then took a long, deep breath with a deep personal prayer. He wiped away the tears with his right hand, opened his eyes and looked over and around the sanctuary, and whispered to himself something he remembered reading some ten years earlier.

"If it takes only one to be bad, logic tells me it also takes only one to be good. That is good news."

Then he spoke those words again to the burgeoning group of people in the sanctuary. Coy looked around the sanctuary and at the small simple box that held Growler's remains. He spoke with his perfectly copied Growler diction and said,

"Pastor, God bless you! You now know you have spent time with your earthly father. He had reason to protect his identity. It is regretful, and I am saddened you have lived your life not really knowing the true identity and what had happened to your father. Praise God you now have answers. Some folks live their whole lives and spend much time with their fathers and never really know them. So, take heart. Furthermore and most importantly, after I think back to my time with your father both in person and reading his book, I know in all my heart, soul, and mind he loved and cared for you very much and is very pleased you know our eternal Father, God."

Coy stopped for reflection and took the few steps towards the pastor and his family and said, "I pray and hope each and every one of you write this on the back cover of the book, which reveals who you are."

Coy paused and took the book he had in his right hand and turned it over to the back cover. He read out loud in his own clear diction, "Take time to appreciate the moments for they will soon be memories. One lifetime is not enough." Coy handed Growler's book to the pastor and said, "God bless you. This is your book now." The pastor was gracious and grateful. Coy said, "I know you will read it carefully, and you will get to know and understand your father or at least a glimpse. Words from and of a man can be a revelation." They hugged each other heartily, realizing a lifetime shared.

Printed by BoD in Norderstedt, Germany